# The Journey

Kaneil Harrison

# DEDICATION

I dedicate this book to Clementine.

# Contents

# Acknowledgments

I would like to express my sincere gratitude to my friends and family for the continuous support. Many people have abandoned me throughout my life's journey, and I'm forever grateful for the people who stick by my side, through thick and thin. To my parents, Karlene and Neil Harrison, I love you, and I hope you guys are proud of me. *The Journey* would be impossible without my parents. I thank God for the strength and courage to complete such a feat.

# Chapter 1: Passport

*Warder, devil, rats, evil, diaper, amaroid, and sued.* You can skip this ad in four, three, two, one seconds. Skip ad. I grew up poor. I was severely beaten as a child. I was raped by a family member at nine years old. Necessities were a farfetched dream. I found utopia through my mother's welfare. My mind often travels to places that my feet can't visit. I am also a deceptive liar. The above statements are not true. Does this disrupt your mood toward the author?

Picasso and Michelangelo make life worthwhile through the gallantry of a gallery. The first and only piece of art I ever purchased was by an unknown artist. It just had a different perspective. The painting was a bird with black dots on its wings.

There was a sun in the background. The picture was remarkably obscure. It gave me a neurological orgasm. There was just a cipher about the imagery, so I bought it. Looking at the painting microscopically, I realized that the dots on the bird's wings had numbers. It seemed that the dots created a map. The numbers were one to three hundred on each side. I followed the pattern and drew profusely. After combining six hundred dots, I still did not understand the map. After several hours of analytical efforts, I realized it was not a map. If you cut the painting in two and put the wings against each other, the dots create a face. This face was Oprah Winfrey. Now substitute almost all the *I*s in the first paragraph, except the sentence of a deceptive liar, with "Oprah Winfrey."

A fantastic illustration. I merely orchestrated a

complexly odd scenario, only to make the point that Oprah Winfrey was the victim in the first paragraph. Why? Oprah Winfrey has absolutely nothing to do with this book, but I want you to grasp the concept that it is okay if you think differently. It is okay if you are different. Not because a person does something entirely beyond the norm, he or she is weird. It is okay if you awkwardly uniquely explain. We all emerge from all walks of life. Meaning we all come from different backgrounds and philosophies, so ultimately we all are different.

Sometimes *Homo sapiens* can be classified as hypocrites. Humans, in general, like to point out what's wrong in other people's life, but when it comes to self, that no longer applies—instead of seeing a smoker as a smoker or a homeless person as a homeless. How about trying to cultivate people's interests through their passion? Rather than slandering the negative things they do, you can transform their passion into business acumen, regardless of the type of passion. For example, a child who may be considered as a "bump" (a worthless person) because he or she plays video games all day. As a parent, you can channel that child's passion into probably the video-game industry. Playing games may lead to a career in software engineering, product development, or game design. The problem and solution are in home upbringing. A tree can't grow at all without roots. Reassess the way you analyze situations. Challenge your thinking mechanism to avoid critical-thinking errors. Try to develop an expertise to cope with essential fears of thinking. Society may produce people with different attributes and characteristics, but there is always a place for you on *The Journey.* This book accommodates everybody. Welcome! All I'm doing is tricking the mind and tweaking the way you think. Technically speaking, an argument could be made that the configuration of the face elicit how tough a childhood Oprah lived, but the bird (Oprah) still manages to fly to the sun (success), but let's not go into that. Let's move back to where we started. *Warder, devil, rats, evil, diaper, amaroid, and sued.* Do you remember these words? What do you see when you look at these words? A warder is associated with a prison. A devil is a demonic serpent. Rats are usually associated with snitches. Evil is synonymous to wicked. A diaper is associated with manure. An Amaroid is a bitter vegetable. Sued is bringing charges against someone. A healthy brain may perceive these words as negative words. They in fact may be harmful words, but look again. What do you see? *Warder, devil, rats, evil, diaper, amaroid, and sued.* How about changing your perspective by looking at the words differently?

Try spelling the words backward. The results will encompass the following: *redraw, lived, star, live, repaid, diorama,* and *deus.* You now realize that these are all positive words. To redraw is an inclination of trying again. Lived means to capitalize on the fact of remaining alive. Stars are luminous spheres that bring forth light. To live is to embrace life. Repaid can be seen as paying back someone you owe. A diorama is a beautiful painting. Deus is Latin for God. This illustration relinquishes that behind any wicked proceedings that occurs in your life, if you look carefully, you can find good from inside.

For some of you readers, the above information so far may not make any sense and is unrelated to the book, but that is okay. In fact, perfect. I am trying to prepare you for the journey ahead. Reading the words above is a training course, exercising the brain to see the proximities of new perspectives and divergent thinking. Challenge your mind to the stage of an enhanced, inevitable, and imaginative experience. Sometimes when you click a video on YouTube, it ends up showing an advertisement. See the content so far as an advertisement. Are you ready for The Journey?

A conversation was with a mirror. Twelve o'clock at night, Budapest, Hungary, a man points anticlockwise at the polished metal and starts to draw covertly with the contours of his face. He stares scrupulously at the task at hand. He asked the mirror the following questions: "Why is it that there is so much money in this world but still people are suffering? Why are dogs living better than some human beings? Why is a struggle an immutable characteristic? Why don't we love anymore? Why?" Then came water protruding from the outskirts of the mirror onto this man's face. I woke up in a rebarbative sweat. It was a dream. A weird dream. At first, the dream didn't make any sense, like a psychopath using a paintbrush to brush his teeth. Sometimes we fail to recognize ourselves, even in our dreams. For several weeks the dream baffled me. However, I came up with a few rationalizations. The twelve o'clock represents dark times in my life, being that it's midnight. The location Hungary is pseudocode for hungry, which expresses the real times I was hungry throughout life's journey and my hunger for success. Despite the emptiness and dark times, I will find myself through life (the mirror), hoping for a positive light. My rationalizations may be wrong. Life is a cycle. Life is hard. Life is a journey, and this is my journey.

All my life I have been trying to figure things out. I had so much bottled-up emotions. The only ammunition I had left was putting pen to paper. Never once thought that writing a book would be my solution. I was never good at English. Seven years ago, I did an English Caribbean exam in tenth grade. Caribbean students are required to take this huge test. I got a grade three for this review. In American terms, a three is probably equivalent to a C or D letter grade. I was ridiculed, jeered, and teased. In the initial stages of writing this book, dozens of people told me that there were too many grammatical errors and the writing lacked spark. I once watched the Brazilian Roberto Carlos score a goal. As his left foot trigger hit the mantle of the ball, it curved rightward toward the goalkeeper. In a series of events, the ball switches and turns leftward defying the laws of Newton, hitting the back of the net like a hellacious knife through scared butter. It was after that moment I realized anything was possible. So I created *The Journey*. I decided that I will never let a negative remark block my capacity to be someone or produce something. However, my escapades are often my encumbrances and vice versa.

I think the most potent weapon in the universe is your mind—a very combative tool, and it is more efficient than any sharp object. If you pour Heineken or Effen Vodka into a glass, don't expect to taste lemonade or a strawberry beverage when you drink from that glass. In other words, what you feed your mind, you naturally become a reflection of it. Nobody can imprison your mind, no matter the circumstances. If you genuinely believe in your ideas and passions, it will come to light once you work hard and maintain discipline.

As readers, by this time you might be asking the question, "What is the journey about?" Before we embark on the journey, two items are required into your suitcase: a new perspective and a passport. The contents might seem light weighted, but the value is corpulent.

I am assuming now you have already gained insights of having a new perspective. To further equip the contents from a fresh perspective, try attempting to find the answers to the questions in the dream, and also try to challenge your comfort zone level. The answers will prepare you for our final destination: Clementine. To be able to travel with me throughout this book, a basic comprehension of my personality is required. The passport of *The Journey* is in my persona. Now, who is Kaneil?

In 1995, my parents Karlene and Neil Harrison gifted me with the blessing of a name. They combined the "Ka" from my mom and added it on to the "Neil" of my dad, to make it "Kaneil."

My name, "Kaneil" is a brand that extremes in fortune, health, and spirituality; very realistic, idealistic, and intuitive. I strive for excellence and use my leadership qualities for the betterment of humanity and not for self-glorification. My goal is to help others and to diminish their deepest fears.

Operating on the spiritual side of my individuality exalts me to a high altitude. I'm a firm believer in God and won't neglect my spiritual identity. I always look for an opportunity to investigate the anonymous, to use and show my mental abilities, and to find the purpose and meaning of life. I aspire to grow wise. I also want to understand people and things. Sometimes I need privacy to replenish energy.

An uncut version of myself can be found in the things that I like. It's the Nelco side of things. Nelco is my alias. I love East Indian mangoes, blended granola punch, Manchester United, and Jamaican cuisine. If I picked an excellent day, it would be a day eating fried chicken and rice and peas with a lot of gravy, playing dominoes with some friends, and listening to some reggae music on a veranda. I also enjoy spoken word poetry at late nights. Spoken word is an art form that is created differently from a regular poem. It reveals a person's innermost emotions.

In every situation, there is usually a home where antonyms resides. For example, an alkaline battery possesses the characteristics of a negative and a positive side. As it pertains to life in general, you have love and fear.

The root of our concerns can be found most times in our childhood experiences. I have an undiscerning fear of dogs and doctor's offices. When I was a baby, it would take hours for me to comply with immunization shots. Where I am from dogs are not pets. They are aggressive creatures, and if you hear a bark that signifies that, you must run. At a young age, I got locked up in a bathroom for thirty minutes because of a faulty doorknob, and that experience triggered my fear of elevators or any enclosed spaces. My biggest fear engulfs any possibility of losing my parents.

Blending the two fruits of life (what we love and what we fear), are all a part of a daiquiri, that I call family—a sweet but strong cocktail. A family is an essential aspect of The Journey. The blessing of a family came in the format of a nuclear family. My father is a track coach back home at a top high school. A very courteous humble man. From my very first step outside the womb, I knew that I could become anything because of my father's constant reminders. My father always holds the profound ideology that his boy was abnormally smart. He emphasizes that the very first sign of heaven is through a woman's beauty, and I should never lay my hands on a woman. I should treat them with respect, care, love, and compassion. My mother is a bank manager who genuinely has a rich smile and a passion for people and life. She always told me that I should never forget where I'm coming from and I should never bite the hands that fed me. Also, I have a beautiful little sister Nekalia. She is the epiphany of a princess.

I was never rich, but also I was never poor. My

parents would go to the extreme just to make sure that my sister and I were okay.

On numerous occasions, I knew that they were struggling, but they still found a way to provide, even under extenuating circumstances.

The broader spectrum of the family including cousins, uncles, and aunts are all comedians. Not regarding job statuses but personalities.

In the corporate world, where ethics is a concern, you have a galore of theories and philosophies. Under the rubble of these methods and philosophies, lies the clash of ethical systems. The clash of ethical systems facilitates an individualistic (business) and a collectivistic (government) approach. For example, sometimes pharmaceutical companies (business) will go to the extreme to promote certain drugs through advertisement, even if the medicine is bad for you, just to make excessive profits. The Food and Drug Administration (government) would then perform its role. They intervene as the bigger person and try to regulate the corporate environment. This intervention will cause a clash or a rift between business and government. In a particular way, this has been the story of my life. Before a child leaves the womb, parents already have an innate description of what they want their child to become. However, when the child gets older, this often gets entangled with what the child actually wants to become, and it creates a clash of ethical system between child and parent. What you didn't know is that I am an athlete and I once owned the honor of representing my country in both soccer and track. Life is all about decisions, and one of the hardest decision I ever made was choosing between two sports. Should I sacrifice myself to be a next person's hero (track)? Or should I be fearless and follow my dream (soccer)?

My first love was at the age of three years old. Her name was Rebecca. Rebecca was a soccer ball. I made sure I handled her with care, delicate touch, and charisma. Rebecca was my passion. At an early age, I knew what I wanted to become. My first ever essay was about, "What do you want to be in the future?" I ultimately wanted to become an international soccer player, playing for FC Barcelona.

The birth of my passion for soccer comes from my first encounter with watching the Samba Boys—the Brazilians. Since I grew up with my dad, I often heard beautiful stories of Brazilian players.

He spoke about Zico, Dunga, Bebeto, Josimar, Romário, and the famous Pele. That tweaked my interest to a superlative level. However, as a young boy, I fell in love with the four R's: Ronaldo, Rivaldo, Roberto Carlos, and the sensational Ronaldinho.

There was just something about the way they maneuver a piece of leather for ninety minutes across the pitch with class, desire, flair, rhythm, and elegance. The English created soccer, but the Brazilians perfected the art. It is true poetry in motion.

After playing a high-school soccer game. At thirteen years old, my living room was bombarded with a Serbian soccer scout.

My family and I had to make a choice. The offer was going to an international school in Serbia while playing soccer. Then the following year, I would transfer over to Chelsea Academy, playing football in England. We had three days to make such a life-changing decision. I would travel from my home country to Sao Paulo, Brazil—how ironic—and then to Belgrade, Serbia. The sports agency alluded the fact that I would be getting a monthly stipend, a stipend that was significantly higher than the salaries of prominent businessmen in my home country. This was the ultimate dream. However, do you know the threshold of such information? My parents ultimately said no, as they felt it was too much of a drastic change and it was too sudden. It was hard for my mom to send her "baby" to a foreign country and let a complete stranger take care of her proudest possession. In life, we can't afford to live with regrets. Maybe if I went to

Serbia, yes, my life would be completely different, but I appreciate the now. The people whom I have met and the experiences gained—not going to Serbia made it all worthwhile. It may be a blessing in disguise. The journey of it all enlightens us of our character and enables self-realization, which ultimately leads to self-growth. Self-realization can be a hell of a drug. The opportunities from the "high" make it all worth it, but the side effects may leave you all alone. How did I begin running?

September 2004. Take your right hand and cover your left eye. Then take your left hand and cover your right eye. "Now, what did you see?" You should be able to see an opaque image. *Darkness*. A domino screen without the white. That was the essence of September 2004. I was nine years old, living in the Caribbean. My family and I were devastated by a category 5 hurricane—a monstrous force of wind and rain exceeding 156 miles per hour (mph). At the time my father was overseas working in Turks and Caicos, so he wasn't present during the hurricane. We had to evacuate during the hurricane because the house was in deplorable conditions and our life was at risk. There was too much water coming in, and the roof was gone. Filled with fear and scattered emotions, as a family, we had a perilous feat ahead. The hurricane was a pestilent child. We had to evacuate. The nearest available shelter was three miles away. During the hurricane, I had to run three miles, holding my baby sister, and it was at that moment I knew I could run. I hated it, but I knew I had some speed. "Can you imagine running in a hurricane while protecting your baby sister and mother, at nine years old?" We lost everything, even "Rebecca." We had nothing left but ourselves. We were homeless for three months. Not homeless, but we didn't have our place. We lost our home. Desperate times call for drastic measures. My parents devised a plan so that we could stay with a family friend. We were going through dark times, and at night it was dark because the entire town didn't have electricity. Two months without electricity. But remember, a family is a strong cocktail, and a family that prays together will stay together. The song writer said we stand together through sunshine and the rain. So from an early age, I had to learn how to adapt to an unforeseen situation. I know what it is to have nothing, so I am grateful for everything.

After five years of built-up assets, hard work, and dedication, my parents were able to purchase land and build a house. The income my parents were gaining in the early 2000s wasn't able to transcend to that sort of standard of living. That is why my dad was working in Turks and Caicos, to ensure a better life for his family. He came back home after five years. There was a lot of talent in Turks and Caicos, but there was no system in place to harness those abilities. So my dad brought back a few Turks and Caicos athletes with him. All of them I consider as brothers. One of them is now a British Olympian, and another is my collegiate roommate.

When my father came back, he realized that I had extraordinary speed. He witnessed that through soccer games. There was no one who could convince me to do track. I hated running. One summer my father told me I was going to do track and that I can't let my talent go to waste. I told him no and that I wanted to play soccer. Even though I told him no, he said that there was track training the next day morning. I stormed outside the house in anger and anguish. My dad ran me down. He held me with a definite purpose and told me that I didn't have a choice. For days I wouldn't talk to my father. One year later I was the fastest fourteen-year-old in the world, with a time of 11.10 seconds. It was only my first year doing track, and I won the 100 m at the national high-school championship. I fell in love with track, but soccer was always my first love. This goes to show that sometimes parents know what's best, even though as a child we can be extraordinarily stubborn.

During my last year of high school, I did not play soccer because of the organization. They were corrupt. A lot of negative influences and outside forces started dictating how we should play soccer as kids. They were like remotes. I did not want to be a part of anything that was negative. So during my last year of high school, my focus was utterly track. An unfortunate situation. If I were at any other high school, I would have played soccer for them. Father didn't enforce the decision. The soccer environment in my high-school system was toxic. When I was younger, we as a high-school team were undefeatable. We used to win every single competition, but when we got older, a lot of outside forces started getting involved. So it wasn't fun anymore. As babies, we were not inflicted by the toxins of this world. You see, as a child, everything is in its innocence. Very uncomplicated, everything is in its purest form. As we grow old, things change, and the innocence starts to decay, because we get exposed to different contents of the world.

After my fourteen-year-old debut on the track circuit, I had extensive amount of injuries. I pulled my two hamstrings, and I had a major growth spurt. Due to the growth spurt, my hips suffered tremendously. As a result of this, I had to switch events from the 100 m to the 400 m. I was very injury prone, and my dad thought that I could handle the less explosive sprint. My last year in high school, I recovered from all of that drama. So it was time to be a reflection of the talent and the hard work. Not playing soccer gave me a chance to see if this track thing could actually work out. My dad was my coach and anything he said I believed. We worked day and night assiduously on the goal ahead.

The goal was to go forty-five seconds and gain a

collegiate scholarship to the United States. Why the United States of America? Not that I have anything against my own country, but my dream was always to go to school in America. I realized from an early age just the fact that you are born in another country put you at a significant advantage not to struggle. I saw America as a great window of opportunity toward a better life. I wanted to be the change of my generation, so that everybody who comes after me would be financially stable.

So my father and I plotted. My first race of my high-school season went significantly well. A lot of colleges were interested. As the season progressed, I started getting faster and faster. However, after a major track meet, I fell out of a bus on my back. I had a slight case of scoliosis, and that accident severely ruptured my back. I had to do many x-rays and try to heal my back. I just wasn't the same athlete anymore. That incident diminished the rate of collegiate offers significantly. However, there was always one recruiter who was still interested. By now you have gained the insights of a new perspective and have equipped the intangible passport via my upbringing (personality). Now it's time to gain the real passport with a visa because I'm going to the United States.

Let's take a break from The Journey by lightening up the atmosphere with a secret. Sometimes when you travel, you might need a snack. Consider this as your snack time or just a good intermission. I also feel as if, if I reveal a secret, you will be able to trust your author. "Can I be real with you?" I told you about my first love but, "what about my second love?" The first girl I ever sincerely love was...

Apparently, I changed my mind. This is not TMZ; this is *The Journey*. So please try and get a physical snack. I have a few recommendations: gummy bears, donuts, Oreos, Doritos, chips, and so on. I want you to mostly get up from this book and soak your mind in some refreshment.

I take it by now that you are more refreshed and ready to engage in *The Journey*. Now, fasten your seatbelts!

# Chapter 2: The Transition

Ladies and gentlemen, welcome aboard *The Journey* Airline, flight 22 student-athlete experience, bound for Manhattan Kansas, with continued service to Clementine International Airport. All pieces of baggage should be stored securely either in an overhead bin or under the seat in front of you to eliminate distractions of you reading this book. All electronic devices should be turned off and stowed away, because they may interfere with your attention span. Sir and Madam, I repeat, please put your cellular devices in book mode. Please review the book information at the back of the book.

This is your author speaking with just a little book information. We will be flying at an altitude of thirty thousand words. Please expect heavy turbulence across the chapter "Kaniel Outis." On routing to "The Cliff," please expect scattered showers. We should reach our destination around two hundred pages. Thank you. Sit back, relax, and enjoy the book.

It seems as if I have a flustered mind. 3:30 a.m., 4:50 a.m., 8:15 a.m., 9:30 a.m., 2:45 p.m., and 6:26 p.m. I have no idea what day is today. Maybe it's the day after Thursday. Nothing comes to mind. This is the point where I am expected to stop. Waiting in vain for a substantive thought. Deep thoughts erupt from indisputable passions. Conniving experiences collage egregious thoughts. I have no thought patterns. I am suffering from lack of thought. I am suffering from lack of sleep. I am trying to fix my mind, like Will Smith in *Collateral*

*Beauty.* Is it safe to say that I have a new brain? There is nothing worse than an irrational decision, except no thought. Am I okay? Do I have a blank mind? I wish that the meditation of my heart could perfume new perspectives in your cerebral sanctums. It is like I am consciously living, but I am in a coma. My sclera is wide open, but my brain is bankrupt.

Then 6:27 p.m. happened. Ideas kept flowing like the river Nile, with the brain igniting thoughts like Nicaraguan volcanoes. I visualized an ancient Greek woman with a percussion instrument, banging drums on the side of my head. Instead of a headache, the outcome was an outpour of thoughts. Lubricated bicycle chains showcased a range of movement, like the ball-and-socket joint. The chains were in synchronization when the cyclist pedals, and this constructs kinetic energy so that the bicycle can move forward. A transition can be a beautiful experience propelling you forward like lubricated bicycle chains. The reaction of the movement is the opposite of potential energy, but the irony gives you great potential moving you forward.

The difference between no train of thought and actual thought was complicated and confusing. Then it is safe to say that transition can also be hard. Things become blurry when you're in transition, like the area in between two paragraphs.

Due to the uncertainty of transition, faith can become an illusion. The more important a call or action is to our soul's evolution, the more resistance we will feel toward pursuing it. According to Rupi Kaur, a Canadian author, "Your art is not about how many people like your work, your art is about if your soul like your work. It's about how honest you are with yourself, and you must never trade honesty for relatability."

Honestly, I have put my heart in this book. *Mi Corazon.* The words are my ventricles, connecting panorama to the reader's mind. Throwing my heart into this book may have repercussions, but you can never erase truthful soul for propaganda.

See the book as an anatomy with a disease but a dichotomy between old and new perspective. The word "between" is the essence of transition— Parkinson's disease to be exact. Meaning I hope the book will have the ability to shake your perception of life, instead of the nervous system.

Sitting under a canopy so Mommy can be happy, thinking about the American dream. In a third-world country, thinking about first-world ideas. An economy of self comes to mind, not wanting the recession of life. As a kid, heaven was on the highest zenith, and right below that, there was America.

The best way to describe how I visualize the American dream was that the things that I saw on television were not tangible. We only could dream of such things. A small-town boy looking to be a mundane hero. I had big problems but big dreams. Where I am from hopes and dreams are dormant, extinct for some. Sometimes castrated by the government. Necessities are sometimes a farfetched dream, much less wants. Things are hard, and the youths are alienated.

Back home we only can dream. Well, I imagined a world of college and Division 1 sports, an outlet for a better tomorrow. A world of a free tertiary education.

This is the point where I introduce the recruiter who made a student-athlete experience possible. The transition can be expressed as a point where having a different background and culture can be a blessing and a burden at the same time. Having to adapt to a new foreign environment is not easy, especially with having no friends or family.

It's like blue and green, having to get along with pink and orange. Apples having to coexist with eggs. A turning point. A crossroad that illustrates something different that can be stupendous but an enormous challenge.

The normal definition of a recruiter as it relates to college and Division 1 sports, is a coach who scouts out the best possible high-school talents to aid one's program, usually toward championships. The recruiter I met was more than that. He came in the form of a father figure. He often shares stories of fighting bears and lions.

A quite charismatic personality, we knew as athletes his stories were untrue. However, we gave him the benefit of the doubt. I think indirectly his story held some sort of grounds in a figurative sense.

Personally, I think he has been fighting off bears and lions in the lives of student athletes. This recruiter, six foot in stature and bald-headed, is imperative in the transition phase of my journey.

The level of respect I have for him is something, I think, he will never know. I think he will never understand. It is unexplainable! He changed my whole life. He gave me the opportunity of a full-scholarship running track at Kansas State University.

He made a dream tangible. I think he believed in my unorthodox running style, which brings tears to my eyes, knowing that he believed. The day I was born was the best day of my life; the day the recruiter gave me the opportunity of a scholarship was the second-best day of my life.

I think there is no way possible I can repay him, but show him gratitude.

I pray to God that Vincent live a long healthy life, and I wish him God's richest blessings. Yes, his name is Vincent Johnson. His name originates from Latin, meaning "conquering." The opportunity he gave me, made this journey a possibility to conquer.

The recruiter epitomizes a moment of transition.

What I now learned is that transition is uncomfortable. People don't normally react well with change; they normally have anxiety or an apprehension. When people usually fly into a new city, the first thing they usually do is check into their hotels because there is that need to get acclimated to find that solidarity or that common place because they are in a new environment.

To leave friends and families in my home country, Jamaica, was very hard. Even though blessed by the opportunity, the transition was hard.

Where I'm from is a beautiful place. One of the most scenic country in the world. Jamaica, land of wood and water. It is said that Jamaicans are one of the happiest set of people in the world. In Jamaica, we have a word we call "vibes"; it is a feeling of joy, laughter, niceness, and positive vibration.

Jamaica has a very esoteric culture—meaning you have to live it to fully understand it. If you take away the vibes, you kill us. Something as simple as a person's shoes or even a piece of bottle, Jamaicans can use it and express it creatively. The people just maintain a certain joy in them. Some of those same people jumping up at parties don't even have food for tomorrow, but all of that get lost in the moment. Even though it is a very beautiful place, opportunity is a scarce commodity.

So the opportunity of a free education and also the chance to be able to showcase my athletic prowess was a life-changing dream.

Not knowing what to expect and not knowing the next move can introduce fear. Fear of lack of growth. The recruiter eliminated all of that, and made Kansas State University a reality. He made things transparent; never once did he ask for my personal best times. He just saw my talent and wanted to invest and inspire.

It was four years ago, but I remembered my parent's inducements before I went to college. In the words of my mother: "Be strong and be polite! Spread your bed and live a clean healthy lifestyle. Do not take anything for granted. Appreciate your blessing. Never sell out for vanity. Materialistic things are not important. Treat people good and respect yourself. God will lead the way, and never forget your roots." Prior to college my mother looked me into my eyes passionately and said, "No matter what you're going through, or no matter how hard it is to tell me, I will never judge you or forsake you. You are my child, which means you are a part of me, which means I am you. I will always be there for you."

In the words of my father: "Kaneil, you're a smart boy, and I know you will make intelligent decisions. You will be successful. Just deal with things and mash up the track."

I am so glad for the way I was raised. A lifestyle filled with great morals and values that I will never depart from. If I could be half the persons my parents are, then I am already successful.

Close the book, look at the cover; I beg you to look into my eyes and let me tell you my story. Smile with the world, hope it wish the best for me. One backpack, one suitcase, one-hundred-dollar bill, and one dream was all I ever had, heading to Kansas State University. It was the late summer of 2013. My family dropped me off the airport, and I am an adult now. Must figure things on my own.

Do you know Walter Rodney and Walter Boyd? First and foremost, they have no direct relation in terms of family ties or with the book. Just bear with me for a second. One is dead, and one is living. One is Guyanese, and the other is Jamaican. Walter Rodney played a pivotal role in Guyana's independence. Walter Boyd played a pivotal role for the Reggae Boyz, scoring against Mexico in the Azteca. Now, we can come to a concise decision and agree that they both played pivotal roles. The thing about pivotal roles is that, it comes with pressure and oftentimes creates controversy.

Walter Rodney was assassinated, while Walter Boyd was alienated. Don't focus too much on the comparison. The comparison is there to educate. See it as a form of a history lesson. Instead of the comparison, focus on the commonality. Black. They are both black men. I want you to focus on the ideology of how a journey can be transcended.

I mean, we live in a world where black is not seemed to be beautiful anymore. It is hidden behind curtains. Nappy hair is subjective to bad, and even a silhouette is black. Even a vulture is black. I once watched a set of black birds. Unfortunate, but it seems as if the birds see lucidity in society's negligence. A world where black birds soar to stadium lights instead of skyscrapers. Synonymous with how black people settle to mediocrity.

We should be proud and embrace who we are. Black, blue, or white, we are all beautiful. Coming from a hemisphere of Marcus Garvey, Mohamad Ali, Madiba, Martin Luther King, and Bob Marley; a heritage of Congo drums and Kumina; a land of sugarcane, plantains, and ground provisions; a culture of steam snappers with okras, carrots, and crackers. A precious endowment. The African blues. The African rhythm. The African gems. We have the prettiest set of minerals. Sierra Leone has the prettiest set of diamonds. An African vibration is opulent. If I had to ask a bigot a question, this would be my question. "If you are sick in the hospital, and the only thing that can save your life is a black person's kidney, would you die?"

The point I am heading to is that going to a predominantly white school can be scary. As a black boy, you simply don't know what to expect.

Backtracking to fours year ago...it was freshman year. This is where the story of a student athlete unfolds.

People fall in love in mysterious ways, maybe just the touch of a hand. Ed Sheeran was playing on the radio. In an airport shuttle, I sit, thinking. My future lies within a university. Traveling from Kansas City to Manhattan, Kansas. My new home lies in front of my eyes. I see corn, ferns, green, and woodland. First impression was an agricultural state. I guess, Welcome to the Midwest.

I slept for hours because of the hectic schedule, traveling from the Caribbean. When I woke up everything was purple. I saw periwinkles, and finally, a Wildcat nation. Excited and invigorated by the concept of college. Back then I thought college was what I saw in *American Pie* movies. A rude awakening awaited me. Greeted by a collegiate town, the city of Manhattan presents itself. Everybody was friendly, super friendly to be exact. The people greeted me with smiles and hugs.

I used to think that kindergarten teachers were

the most powerful human beings. Thought they possess superpowers like Marvel movies. The reason for that rational is that they have an early opportunity to interact with an infant brain. I thought that a kindergarten teacher position was critical because they give an upcoming generation a mental polygon. My brain was evoked when I saw the number of variety of beautiful college girls in Manhattan, Kansas. They were blondes, brunettes, Asians, and Latinas, to name a few. An environment filled with distractions for the unstable mind. I needed my kindergarten teacher. Of course, I got introduced to Aggieville, a strip of bars and party life, where you see rampant drunk people.

To me at first the university was extremely huge. I didn't have access to a vehicle, so I pretty much walked everywhere. I got lost on so many occasions, running around in circles. For those of you who know Manhattan, I remember walking from Jardine Apartments to Walmart to get groceries. My roommates had cars, but I just didn't like to ask for rides. Don't like to put my burden on another person's shoulder, but I was also aware of the fact that no man is an island. I just decided to do it by myself. I wasn't aware of the bus system because I was fairly new. There was a struggle walking with groceries, and sometimes I just took a taxi back.

Remember days of skyping my family so that I could feel at home. I often tell people not to confuse the silence of my lips with apathy. My family is 1,922 miles away. Nobody to run to but God. Student athletes have the pressure of balance. It's a bicameral world. We must make sure things are okay on both spectrums. As a freshman, I wanted to do exponentially well, academically and athletically. The responsibilities of a student athlete are rigid, to say the least. It is a tough world.

In terms of facilities, it was eye opening and mind grabbing. I had access to three weight rooms. There were fuel stations with Gatorades and shakes. Fruits and sandwiches at your disposal. We had an indoor track and an outdoor track. A pool that was always available. There was a training room with physiotherapist and athletic trainers. Foam rollers and ice baths to prevent injuries. It was top-notch facilities comparing to back home. The athletes and coaches in Jamaica would die for such facilities. So many times, people had asked me the following question: "Why are Jamaicans so fast, especially with such limited facilities?" There is no one answer to that question. Jamaica is an impoverished country. A third-world basin. Personally, I think many youths see track as the way out of a struggle, so little or no resources will not get in their way. Once they have grass and a pair shoes to train, then they are okay. It is an outlet that can provide for the betterment of their families. So knowing that gives them great motivation. Many youths are cognizant of this, so they train very hard. What makes it easy is that Jamaica fosters a culture of track and field, from a very young age, just like how Americans breathe on the culture of football and basketball. Jamaica has the biggest high-school track meet in the world, that magnetizes recruiters from all over the globe. The way you see football stadiums in America, that's how it is at track meets in Jamaica. Many people might say it is the food that we eat or our African genetics.

On an academic basis, they were tutors who were mandatory for incoming freshman. You had academic counselors, and advisers who helped with your class choices and major selection. Also for a freshman, you had to complete mandatory study hours. It was six hours a week. If the hours were missed, you had punishment, and usually you would get a not-so-nice message from coach. The punishment would entail getting up early about 4:00 a.m. and running for hours.

So the stage was set for me to do well and progress. The purple nation was impressive. Sounds like a glorious platform for greatness. Facilities were there for growth. However, let me educate you on the life of a student athlete. I woke up at six o'clock every morning for weightlifting training.

Then, after weights, there was a day filled with classes. After classes I had practice at 4:00 p.m. After a strenuous practice, I would get a quick bite to eat at the cafeteria. Then I had mandatory tutor sessions, that I had to attend and study hours to complete. It was like a never-ending cycle! Eat, sleep, train, study, and repeat. On days that I had no training, I had some type of important meeting to attend. Any little chance I got, I slept. I usually plan on when to sleep, because every second of rest counts. That was my lifestyle. Social life was deprived. At first it was hard to adjust, but that's where discipline comes in to play. There is a Jamaican proverb that goes like this: "If you waan good, you nose haffi run." It means "in order to gain success, you have to work hard." So automatically, everything became a routine. I had a new robotic life, always busy and occupied.

American time is so different from Jamaican time. When the coach says training is at 4:00 p.m., you better be there by 3:59 p.m., or else you're late. Trust me; you don't want to be late. I remember mornings of full-fledged sprinting from my apartment to make it to weight lifting in the mornings. Track and field is a self-discipline sport, and with that comes sacrifices that you must make. You must distinguish priorities from irrelevancies. When you do that, you may lose some people in your life, who don't really understand The Journey. Some of those people may be even family members. I had to be mentally prepared and physically engaged for anything.

The life of a student athlete is unpredictable. You must ensure to take care of your body, to minimize the rate of injuries. Eating healthy and having a balanced diet is critical, along with getting the right proportion of sleep. You can't show up to training tired. A tired person cannot train effectively. At the end of the day, you must make sure things are going well with your classes. A grade point average below a certain level will cause an ineligibility to compete.

One of the hardest things to deal with was switching coaches. That transition was complicated. From a tender age, my dad was always my coach. So to adjust to another coach's teachings and philosophies was extremely hard. The coach I had was a high-jump guru, but I was a 400 m athlete. Our relationship was indecipherable.

I listen to motivation speeches at nights to cope with any unsure thought patterns. Also read my Bible. Ray Lewis said, "Pain is a repetition of the psyche." So I try not to feel pain, even though I was aware of the fact that the days were becoming long and unnerving. I was missing home and my comfort zone. It is good to be uncomfortable. You can't expect great things to come easy. My father used to tell me, "Train hard; then you die."

When I had that thought concept, that is the time when the winter season hit. Coming from a world of tropical marine climate, sunshine and beaches is all that I am accustomed to. There was never a need for jackets, scarves, and gloves in my homeland. In the Caribbean, if we wore jackets, it would be only for something stylish. Coming from the Caribbean, not having many jackets, what I did was, wore many layers. For example, four to five shirts to keep me warm. Prior to Kansas, I have never seen snow in my life. At first it was a beauty. After that it was repulsive. I hated the snow. I remember days of freezing until my fingers became numb. The cold weather was intolerable for this island boy.

It was at that moment everything started to spiral downhill. A new character was born, and you will learn about in the next chapter. I could not keep up with the robotic schedule any further. There were days that I stood up late to complete assignments. The next morning, I arrived at weight lifting as a zombie. Sometimes it would be a multiple choice between sleep, going to class, and training. I had to go to training, or else I would lose my scholarship. On days that I would have three or four classes, I would choose sleep. Unfocused and bewildered.

In the midst of a freshman winter night, about 1:30 a.m., I was sleeping preciously. I heard a loud bang on my room door, and heard the words, "You black nigger, you need to go back to Jamaica!" That was my first racial encounter in Manhattan, Kansas. Suddenly, I thought the people weren't so friendly anymore. In the words of my mother, "All that glitters is not gold." I thought, is this really the American dream? What I didn't tell you guys is that I had an uncomfortable environment. My living situation was a mess. It affected my holistic lifestyle. There were days I would stand outside to hide from the pain. I used to spend hours outside my home, and I was miserable when I went to bed. No matter how talented you are, if your environment is not right, you will not perform well.

I now became a struggling freshman. I was struggling in my classes, got a 1.75 GPA, and was on academic probation. The college of business threatened to kick me out if my GPA was ever like that again. Running slow times, and struggling to have a relationship with my coach. Young, lost, and in a frantic state.

Like fishermen looking at empty nets, my heart was petrified. Mommy calls from a distance, and I don't answer. "How can I tell her that I am failing?" Failing to be the best Kaneil. One of the worst things to hear in life is the disappointment in a mother's voice. When you look at a safari, you see crocodiles, other boats, and the river. What is under the water is so unsure, but the boat that I am in, still manages to float. That's what I try to think about. I have no idea of the direction my life is heading to, but I still lift my head up. One thing for sure, at that point in my life, I hated Kansas. The biggest thing I feared was losing my scholarship. I wasn't performing, and my grades were subpar.

What I saw on television was no longer appetizing. I became blinded and sad; perhaps bitter, young, and naïve. The life of a student athlete has only begun. The life of adulthood has only begun. I was hoping for a change. Change? This was only the genesis of my problems. The tip of the iceberg. Kaniel Outis was born. A cascading series of unbelievable events. Counting from one to five thousand, hoping to find a qualitative solution. I was no longer Kaneil.

Now, we can see the transition, of not only coming from a different place into a new environment but also the transition from Kaneil to Kaniel Outis. A Singapore genius facilitated the comprehensive understanding of solving arithmetic equations. It is said that Albert Einstein possessed a high quality intelligence in the theory of relativity. I am not a Singapore genius or Einstein; however, it's an amicable admiration. "What about the Rhodes scholar?" I am sorry, not Rhodes scholar, but the road scholar. The road scholar or otherwise known as the man in the ghetto with the street smart. That was what I tried to hold on to because apparently the school thing wasn't working out. Don't get me wrong! It is not that I was a dumb child, but I was unfocused in a polluted environment. The thing about being street smart is that you have the ability to improvise, but how can you improvise when things are only getting harder? Everything is against your odds.

I felt like an impoverished, malnourished Muslim, having to make the choice of eating available pork. It's either kwashiorkor or going against a religion. The random shit I think about when my brain has a spasm. On a serious note, do I go back to Jamaica, or do I try to survive?

Instead of using a sinkle bible, I pick up a single bible. But...

# Chapter 3: Kaniel Outis

I once spoke with a pancreatic-cancer patient. He told me that everything was going to be okay. He died the following week. RIP Earl Powell. I once spoke with a neighborhood-community guy; he had ALS disease.

We all know there is no cure for ALS disease. He told me that everything was going to be okay. He died the following month. RIP, Tony Gayle. I once spoke with a street-side higgler, otherwise known as my godmother. She died too. These people were the people I knew; people who were important to me.

This troubled my faith, because all the people who I wanted to help when I became successful was dying. I was wondering why God is doing this. It troubled my faith. I also texted a now dead girl on Facebook, that everything is going to be okay. She had meningitis. I prayed, and she died. I cried and cried. I am searching for something, and my heart is empty, but still I smile. I am searching for an answer. Why bad things happen to good people? Have you ever lost someone so close to you? It is said that God gives the toughest battles to the strongest soldiers.

Have you ever been in a dark room before? There are no windows, and your thoughts are dispersed. Like a nonlinear graph, your thoughts are of a yo-yo. So many variables and equations, just to find $x$. A quadratic equation in life's purest form. Apparently, the dark room is a complicated place. Perhaps, a lonely place. I come to realize when you're on a common course of action in getting a goal, you will encounter many dark rooms. My freshman year was a dark room.

In my home country, you have a term we refer to as "ghetto youth." This is a person who goes through extreme suffering and do not have much necessities, thus extremely poor. There are hundreds of ghetto youths in Jamaica. There are people in Jamaica who don't have mere running water to even take a shower. Jamaica is an impoverished country. This scenario often coincides with the high crime rate. People are suffering, and they literally have nothing. So they think the extreme because they don't have other alternatives to survive. The extreme can possibly result in bank robbery or even killing another person. It's a dog-eat-dog world. A dark room. The epitome of Maslow's hierarchy.

From the above example, we can conclude that the dark room can propel the unthinkable. Let's go back to the first paragraph. Imagine this dark room is located in Sana'a, Yemen. Sana'a Yemen is a Muslim territory with one of the toughest prisons in the world. There are many dark rooms in this prison. In this prison there lies, Kaniel Outis. This is a fictional character in the action-packed drama series, *Prison Break.*

On the periphery of the prison was a city full of scraps of debris. A nicotine environment with promiscuous bombs kissing the terra firma.

Buildings were hard to recognize. The Taliban rules the land over the government. Having a passport was luxury. Leaving the country was like going to heaven. The airport was overpopulated and chaotic. They would slaughter homosexuals, highlighting them as infidels. Guns were toys, and boys were puns. Nowhere was safe. It was like a prison outside of a prison. To get out would be a contradiction. An intolerable environment.

Before Kaniel Outis was mislabeled, untreated, and undesirable, he was Michael Scofield, a character who can unleash the brain power of any virtuoso. A perspicacious personality. In fact, he has always been Michael, but the unfortunate environment portrays him as another person.

Freshman year, I felt like Kaniel Outis, captivated and locked up in a dark place. My experiences as a freshman were horrid. My environment consisted of an alcoholic roommate, racism, and witty jokes. No place to really call home, which deeply affected my athletic performance. I hated Kansas. The change was too drastic, and I wasn't really prepared for it. School was rough, my environment was rough, and my relationship with my coach was sandpaper (not the recruiter). There were days that I broke down and cried; it was unbearable. There were also days that were uncertain. There was nobody to run to.

Turn your lights down low. Turn your lights off. Get a candle. I want you to read this chapter under a dim light so you can walk the same journey. I want you to feel the emotions and bear the pain with me, so that you can have a surreal experience. This chapter cannot be read under a bright light because the words or going through dark times. "Kaniel Outis" signifies dark times in my life—dark times in college, dark times as a human being. Once upon a time, there was nothing such as euphoria. I was once numb. Life was sour and broken.

Sometimes I go to the swimming pool, not to swim but to drown my thoughts. I am drowning. Everything is going wrong, and my faith is troubled in a foreign environment. The harsh reality is that most people don't even know; my problems are anonymous. Nobody knows it but me. Who feels it knows it. Not everybody can walk in my shoes and still survive. Some people in my home country automatically think that I am making money because I am in the United States. A mythical concept. I am only a student athlete on full scholarship. They confuse full scholarship with wealth. I thought hurricane Ivan in 2004 was the last hurricane I had to face. I now must engage with hurricane life battles, a season that seem to be all year round.

I used to think that my grandmother was God. She had supernatural powers. The power to love regardless. Her interior qualities were omnipotent. Quite ubiquitous! Pure and silk like a baby's forehead with Jergens. Everybody has a heart, but not everybody loves. Everybody has sight, but not everybody has vision. My grandmother has everything. When you take away the matriarch, it leaves your family into nonexistence because that's the source. Like the sun is for the earth. Sometimes I know I only survive on the basis of my grandmother's prayers. If I lose her, how am I going to survive?

On a third floor I sit, reminiscing to Brian McKnight and Jagged Edge, thinking about my problems and how I can solve them. The telephone rings, and I answered. I heard the words, "Kaneil, your grandmother is in the hospital!" Tears ran down my eyes like water on a Volvo's windshield. My mind became vacant. I immediately started to ponder, visualizing days when she taught me how to make dumpling. Dumpling is a flat, fried buttery dough. I once bought Kentucky Fried Chicken (KFC) for my grandmother. When I brought it to her, she told me that I was disrespectful and wanted to kill her. I laughed and smiled. In her words, "Kaneil, remember, I have arthritis and diabetes, and I can't manage anything that is fried!" She said, "Kaneil, remember, I am sick." So she gave me back the KFC, and I decided to eat it. While eating it, she looked at me and said, "Beg you a piece!" She took the whole box and ate everything. Grandma was willing to sacrifice her health at the expense of her grandson's happiness. It was as if she appreciated me buying the food for her more than anything else in the world.

Grandma is sick. What can I do from so far away? I put everything on pause or delay, even my classes. Even my well-being. You see, Grandma is the origin. She made it possible for a generation of great morals. That has been passed down the pipeline. Everything my dad, uncle, or aunt represents is a result of grandma's teachings.

The sickness that grandma possess has the ability to dissect the brain, eating it like maggots. My grandmother was slowly forgetting people. Her thought patterns were out of sequence. She had

Alzheimer's, a progressive disease that destroys memory and other important mental functions. She was struggling to get fluid to her brain. The doctors said that they can't do any form of surgery because she already has had two strokes. As we know Alzheimer's has no cure, but the Harrison family has faith regardless of present circumstances. The disease has the tendency for grandma to forget things, but one thing I am sure that she will never forget is, her love for the Lord. Does my grandmother survive? Find out in the final chapter, "Clementine."

Epidermolysis bullosa is an inherited connective-tissue disease causing blisters on the skin. If acquired, with the slightest touch, your skins fall off. My blisters were around my brain and heart, and my world was falling off. I had epidermolysis in my life and not skin. As a track athlete, my habitat is a chevron. Oftentimes the days at the track are accumulated with lactic acid and constant agony. To complete a program, you have to be mentally tough. Most times when I am done with practice, I have to sprint to classes to deal with another agony. One day at track practice, half way through my program, I slightly browsed through my phone. A text message came through. I saw the words, "Kaneil, Mom is in the hospital."

My world significantly broke down. I spoke with God and said to him: this was too much. I thought that he wouldn't give me more than I can bear. So now, both my mom and grandmother were in the hospital. I turned off my phone to hide from all notifications. I migrated from a dark place to a darker place. Remember, I was 1,922 miles away from home. So I couldn't counterattack any pain. That same day I stayed at the track and stared in the sky for hours, trying to make sense of the world.

It seemed as if my mother was on drips so that fluids and medicines can be given directly into her blood via the vein. When my sister was a baby, she had problems opening her eyes. We feared that she was blind. A horrible scare for the family. The family doctor said that my mother should put breast milk into my sister's eyes and she would be fine. She was fine. I am trying to find solace in previous miracles. I finally had the courage to call my mother. She said that the doctors are doing a few tests and she will be okay. I have heard that before, so I was still scared. She came out the next day and started working the next week.

Good to know that my mother was okay.

Grandmother was still in the hospital. My mother called me and asked, "Son, are you okay in Kansas?" I smiled and laughed and told her that everything was great. She asked if I have money. I said yes. She asked if there was food in the apartment. I told her yes. She asked how is track going. I told her it's going wonderful. She said, "Son, are you sure?" It is mother's nature to understand when her child lies or when something is wrong. All my answers were lies. My mother just came out of the hospital, and the last thing I wanted to do was stress her with my problems.

Many days I would go to bed hungry, car tank empty, suffering financially. I get a monthly check from the school, but when you minus rent and taxes because I am international, you barely have anything left. We get breakfast and dinner free, but sometimes you are so busy, you don't even get a chance to go to the cafeteria. Sometimes I save and have adequate cash, but my priorities were in the wrong place at times. Stressful times offer irrational decisions. So I wasted the money. My bank account was more often in the negative than the positive. I remember, one day, my bank account was negative fifty-five dollars, and a childhood friend was in problems back home.

He asked me for some money to help him. I told him that I did not have it. He said that I was lying. He doesn't even

understand the half of it all. There were days I stare

at my computer screen, refreshing the page, hoping that my account balance would change. There were days I went to the ATM, knowing there was no money on the card but still tried to draw money hoping for a miracle.

Remember days of going to buy food, and was greeted with the words, "Sir, your card has been declined." What an embarrassment and predicament to have. Everyone sees what you appear to be, but few experience what you really are. Still I laugh and keep a smile on my face because I am confident of good over evil, and I know nothing last forever. Walking through fire but still we hold on. We hold it like a soldier and brace for a better tomorrow.

What can we gather so far? I am broke, struggling in school, struggling in track, my mother just came out of the hospital, and my grandmother is in the hospital. I am Kaniel Outis.

Collegiate problems were only germinating. I was lost and not taking care of self. I noticed a slight difference in my bodily functions. I was urinating more frequently than often. Every second I wanted to use the bathroom. I went to the urologist and tested my prostate, and everything was okay. Did a few more tests, and the doctors told me that there was something slightly wrong with my kidneys. The creatinine level was abnormally higher than usual. The doctors told me to come back in a month so they can run more tests. I was scared, so I could not wait for a month. So I went to a Jamaican urologist. The first thing she said to me was that my lips looked little dry. Then she asked, "Are you drinking water?" I slowly reminisced, and I could not remember the last time I drank water. Probably more than two weeks. The irony, as I was a track athlete, I was supposed to be hydrating every day. I was so stressed that I forgot to hydrate. That was the problem. I went back and did the tests in a month, and everything was back to normal. I did not tell my family or anyone.

On the same day that Paul Walker (*Fast and Furious* actor) died, I was in a motor-vehicle accident. The taxi man who drove was very drunk. You could smell the alcohol on his breath, and he was rambling with his words. Within minutes, the taxi collided with an SUV, smashing the windows, leaving my body to ricochet off the car seat. I got up and realized that I was still alive. Out of fear, I ran out of the taxi, straight to my apartment, which was a twenty minutes run. I have no idea what happened to the taxi driver or the other driver. I don't even know if the police came. I was so scared but so thankful for my life. When I got to my apartment, I got down on my knees and just started praying.

The accident troubled my sensory neurons. I was shaken up. I had a delayed reaction to certain stimulus, and this affected me tremendously. One of my weaknesses in track was my start. The accident made my start even worse as I had a delayed reaction to the starter gun. Injuries were hell of a thing in college. Right after that I dropped a forty-five-pound weight on my big toe. I could not wear track spikes because it would squeeze my big toe. I could not sprint.

I may get into trouble for saying this, but it is the truth. In terms of team dynamics on the track team then, the environment was controversial. It was a very touchy subject. A delicate issue. I would walk to the track and receive dubious smiles and hellos, knowing that the greeting wasn't genuine. Many times when people ask if I am okay, they just ask on the basis of conversation. They don't really care, because before you even start answering, they already start walking away. It didn't seem as a family to me. You had segregated groups within the team. So going to the track was more like a burden than a home. It didn't feel real. It made everything harder for me. It was something different, because my high-school track team was a family. I went to an all-boys high school. The guy to my left was my brother. The guy to my right was my brother. Going home was a burden; going to the track was a burden. My life was miserable, but my smile was vibrant.

My hands were weak, and the days were long;

with irksome comes a lethargic consciousness. I walked in a grocery store and could feel magnetic eyes on my black skin. It was as if I wasn't supposed to be there. I felt unwelcome and unworthy. I asked myself, is this racism? Thought that it was abolished. But like lines of latitude and longitude on a globe, it's there but imaginary. Tensions arose over the cash register. A Caucasian lady was in front of me, and she needed five more cents to pay for her items. She didn't have her credit card and only had restricted cash. I thought that it was a friendly gesture to give her the five cents. She refused to take it from me and decided to put back down all her items. I may be paranoid, but did she not take the five cents because I was black?

Have you ever been in a situation where a person looks at you and says he or she did not see you? Or, you and a person is texting for days, and when you finally see the person, he or she walks past you or hold his or her head down in his or her phone pretending to text. Is that a level of immaturity or wholesome shyness? Can we attach that stigma to fakeness? There were fake people all around me.

We live in a world where a cynical nature is emphasized. Some people are just all for themselves. Nobody loves anymore. Only a few people really care about you. Unfortunate, but true. Unfortunate, but those people may not include family members. Bishop T. D. Jakes labels the people who will infinitely support you as "confidants." These are people who will stick with you, no matter what. These are the people who love you unconditionally. He said, "If you have two or three confidants in a lifetime, you are a blessed person. Without them you will not find out who you are supposed to be." The Caribbean environment was my confidant in Kansas—an environment that revolutionized my cogitation.

In order to change the trajectory of my life, I needed something new. I needed a system. Thoughts occurred to transfer to a different school, but I hate starting something and not finishing it. I also like challenges. Something with substance was needed. I was searching for something. I was searching for something. I was searching for something. A mickle is the powerful grace that lies in plants, herbs, or stones. Searching for the powerful grace in self.

I was once bald. I made a premeditative decision to grow my hair. Many people asked, "Why did you grow your hair?" Many people wanted me to cut it, including my mother. Maybe after this rationale, she will understand. I often tell people that barbers are expensive in Kansas, but that wasn't the reason. The truth is that I started growing my hair because of the pain I felt as a freshman. My hair is symbolic of strength. Every strand of hair represents a struggle, but it also attests to growth—growth not only in hair but also in character.

Sometimes you must get at your lowest to see God at his greatest. Where do you go when you have nothing left? First thing I knew I had to do was face the truth. Truth is the only thing on this earth that will set you free. You can't hide from the truth. I needed to be cognizant of what was going on in my life and stop feeling sorry for myself. I needed the truth. You have seen these words before, "the Caribbean Environment." This leads to the second thing that I did. I had to find refreshing relationships. Then I had to motivate my life with the three *Fs*. I don't know how it is going to work out, but it's going to work out—faith. Stop worrying about what people think—freedom. Don't be afraid of the future—fearless.

Something to think about. Christians believe that if you don't baptize you cannot go to heaven. So what about the innocent three-year-old baby who's not baptized but gets murdered by the mind of a criminal at gunpoint? Does she not get to go to heaven? Don't get me wrong. I am not questioning God, but I think once your heart is pure, God will know your true intentions. Many people camouflage their intentions through their religious identities. Even some Christians have devilish attributes, pretending that they are holy and pure, but some of their ways are demonic. What about the murderers?

Do murderers get to go to heaven? God says you must learn to forgive. There is no good sin or bad sin. A murderer is the same as a fornicator. The important thing is that we ask for forgiveness and repent. For the nonreligious people who are reading this book, I won't discriminate if you don't believe in God, but you got to believe in something. In other words, what are you living for? As a man, you can't stand for nothing, or else you will lose yourself.

Let's take the *Prison Break* scenario up a notch. Let's relate it to real life. I once watched a documentary. A documentary of a now-grown man who was locked up at thirteen years old. He got 107 years sentence to life in prison. He and his friend went over a house to cut grass, and the person told them that they should leave. They did not want to listen, so the next thing you know it was a double homicide. Homicide is the act of a human killing another. Now locked up in bars for life. One hundred years before parole. He is now thirty-five. He has no idea what the world is. All his dreams have been confiscated by a dumb decision. Ibuprofen can't cure his pain. He has never paid bills, never driven a car. He is a boy in a man's body because he hasn't experienced anything but a jail cell. He is Kaniel Outis 2.0.

How can we relate all of this to The Journey? As a result of dark times, I was Kaniel Outis. I was wondering, Does God still love me? What I found out is that hard times do not define God's love. Sometimes he puts you in a position so that you can understand the journey. You must embrace the journey so that doors can open. Things are hard, but I still stand. Tears doesn't equate to the fact of losing. I am going through an albatross, a psychological burden that feels like a curse.

My future wife, whoever she is, must see me at my lowest. She must understand Kaniel Outis. I want her to love me for me. The good Kaneil, bad and indifferent. I value family, and it would be a blessing if I could have one of my own. I am preparing myself mentally, financially, and spiritually for my future wife, because I understand that before I meet my wife, I must be in a healthy place. So when she sees me, I should be the manifestation of her prayers. At the end of day, pimps have to hang up the jersey. You will need someone to share your success, and that is all a part of the journey.

I started approaching problems like Tomokazu Harimoto smashing Ping-Pong balls—a Japanese wunderkind in table tennis. The Caribbean environment was my first solution. What is the Caribbean environment? Justin Gatlin has a rapport of a cheater. A drug cheat. He is one of my favorite athletes because the odds are always against him. In a nutshell, the Caribbean environment embrace all my odds. It's a superlative humane feeling when other humans synchronize in love and one accord.

One of the best things that could happen to a kid is to have both parents, especially if they are married. You are born into a union. Sounds wayward, but single parenting has become prevalent. So many dads and moms are running from their responsibilities. I always look up to my parents. They have an ardent relationship. So as a kid, my environment was loving. So this Kaniel Outis that I experienced was different. A new territory. I have no family in Kansas. So when I scream in the nights, nobody answers. A man can be discouraged and never tell you. My mind is like a drunken snake. My brain operates like the New Zealand haka. I am lonely. Restoration of the soul is needed. I don't need a default setting.

Being invisible is a luxury of the young. When you are young, your mind is a spaceship. Adrenaline constantly flows. You think that you can conquer anything. When you are young, you also have toys. One of those toys might be pornography. As a man, you may try to medicate your pain through a computer screen, but that is not the solution. You start to solve your problems when you start resisting temptations. Instead of buying fast food, how about cooking. Food for the soul is needed when you are at an intersection, because oftentimes we don't know what to do and we panic. The statement I'm about to say is a life moment in this book. "For every man who waits to quit, you must *fight back*."

I was getting tired of people telling me what I can't do. I needed someone to medicate my pain and tell me what I can do. I was looking for insurance, a sense of comfort, a source of real encouragement. I got to fight back and change my circumstances. All this time I was focusing on the negative. Instead of finding a way to look at the positive, I got caught up in negative times. Dark times can make you blind, and your qualities can become distorted.

Some people believe that problems birth from

previous generations. My great grandfather was probably cutting sugarcane for a slave master. Slaves would go through days of hardship. There was no humanity. If you were born black in those days, it was a disadvantage. My bloodline has always been struggling. The abolition of slavery is a sugarcoat for current problems. At a tender age, my mother lost her parents.

At fourteen years old, she became the mother of her siblings. Those were days of going to school bare feet and walking for hours so they could get water. My father was super talented, but in his days, there were no such thing as scholarship. It may be a blessing in disguise, because if he had got a scholarship to the United States, maybe I wouldn't have born. There are so many variables going into the life of a newborn. So many sperms in the human body. So the fact that you are living is a blessing, even if you're struggling.

No matter how good you try to live, there are going to be folks who hate you. I refuse to give up based on what another person thinks. I refuse to give up. I choose to survive. I decide to give my best regardless. What's the point of succeeding if succeeding is easy?

## Abyss

In the midst of the night,
Searching for blue skies,
Only thing I receive is teary eyes.
Misery running down esophagus,
Hope running up windpipes,
I am stifled by oscillation.
Insulin is needed.
I am a broken pencil,
Cut me down into peace,
Not pieces
Half way through this book, I wonder is this real.
Probably I should stop because nobody will feel
The pain,
The pain of an unsung hero.
God is listening,
But I need fertilizer on my prayers...
Then there was the Caribbean Environment.
A moment of abyss,
A moment of deep connection.

## Chapter 4: Caribbean Environment

The vibes that Keznamdi gives to a reggae beat is the vibes I'm looking for. Got some problems that keep me up like coffee. Got some positive vibes to keep me from the coffin. Need change of building. Need change of scenery. Positively clear like lighting a Chalwa. After my freshman year, I packed my bags and ran. It's time to orchestrate a new environment. An environment with garbage create polluted minds. An oiled sea blasphemed the minds of streamline creatures. Rumor has it that the best weed is Jamaican. Never smoked in my life, but I have a high on thoughts. I felt like a soldier coming home from Iraq. I was changing my life.

Taking away some of the pressure that you might have encountered with the previous chapter. A woman is so beautiful. Her regime is magnificent. The trouble that a guy goes through for a girl he likes is alluring. When I like a girl, I can't sleep. Invictus is sprayed onto shirt. Hair is well groomed. Shoes are laced onto feet entrancingly, because she must see me in my element. It is so daunting when you make all the right moves and it goes unrecognizable. It's like losing a lung. A man protecting a woman is like a Nigerian general protecting his army. To find a wife is a good thing, but to find a positive environment is a great thing.

Now back to schedule. A positive environment is very important for your growth and development. However, a toxic environment can help recognize what you need to change as a person. The motive was to find 360 degrees. A new circle, a new clique, a new home, create a system of stability. When you have good people around you who can uplift you, you are already successful.

The laceration of an environment can expose how it affects people in it. In Jamaica, you cannot be openly gay. Jamaica is a very homophobic country. Sodomy is not tolerated. The possibility exist that you will be stoned or beaten. The concept is more skewed toward gays, because if lesbians are walking on the streets in Jamaica, nobody says anything. The double standard of it. So it's an intolerable environment for homosexuals.

You have people in this world fighting for wealth, power, and prestige. People with mansion and luxurious cars, the upper-class hierarchy. Then you have people in the ghetto who are suffering. They have a financial burden. It amazes me to see young mothers having more babies when they are not financially stable. So this means two things: they are not educated on the usage of contraception or the only thing that is fun for them is sexual intercourse. Due to a struggling ghetto with a pugnacious environment, crime rate goes up.

Just bear with me for a second. Exploring different environment to see how the world works, before we go into my specific environment. The world creates a balance through contrasting environment. It's like a seesaw effect. I just think that there is way too much money in this world for people to be poor. I want you to know however the environment you were born in doesn't stop the potential for you to be great. Open your eyes. There are so many superstars who originate from rough beginnings. Your story is on the onus of you.

The Caribbean Environment. This was my safe

heaven, where all my problems were diminished. This was my hiding place. The environ was a place of consolidation that protected me from Kaniel Outis. It is a gargantuan task to have peace during affliction. The Caribbean environment manufactures a level of sanity and solidarity behind my present circumstances. "Do you know how good it feels to actually call a home, a home?" Many people out there are living in homes, but they are not actually at home. Meaning, there is a level of unhappiness. The home is toxic with bad relationships.

Some relationships nowadays are surviving just on the basis of the amount of years in them. "Is your home really your home?" Or is it just a place that you reside? A place where you just put your head on a pillow is not a home. Sometimes a home can be devastated with abuse, infidelity, and neglect. Couples try to endure their relationships through their kids and prior great experiences. You can't sacrifice your happiness at the expense of someone else. You can't sacrifice your happiness because of ego either. Sometimes you have to step outside the box and hydrate your thoughts so that you're not blinded by the misconception of just a piece of building being a home. A home represents more than that equation. It represents a family not necessarily by blood, but a place where a group of individuals can grow and learn from each other through good levity. The Caribbean environment is indeed my home. The ramification of bad times is normally an alcoholic drink, whether brandy, vodka, tequila, or rum. Just something that can drink away the pain/sorrow and soothe the problems away. Luckily my rational was positive through my Caribbean environment. Coach Johnson represents The Transition, while the Caribbean Environment represents a skeletal system—my backbone!

The Caribbean environment coincides with three elements: 324-F, brethren, and sisters.

Some of you might be wondering, what the hell is 324-F? The concept originates from my apartment number. It is simply my apartment. The number 324-F is a legacy and a dynasty in itself. The memories built in 324-F compensates a lifetime of future great experiences. I could die tomorrow and feel great, knowing that I truly lived in 324-F. The memories will never evade into an unfamiliar diaspora. The relationships gained and maintained there is a game breaker. Regardless of your demographics, skin color, status quo, or religion, this is a place where *anyone* can come in and have a slice of cake, devour some serious Caribbean food, and also be able to quench a strong soursop juice.

It is my Sessame in Kansas. It is the "crib." It is an occasional party hub. It is my home away from home. It is a lifestyle. More importantly this is where I gained three brothers. A brotherhood was established. Each brother has an unbelievable trait. A certain DNA unique characteristic that add flavor to 324-F. Their unique attributes add spice to the soup.

The first brother is a bit of a blender, not in terms of sexuality, but place of origin. He originates from Canton Mississippi. He was born in Georgia but is Jamaican at heart. As a matter of fact, Devie Freeman has a big heart. Some people may not like him because of his frank personality. Sometimes in life what is always on the surface is not necessarily true. Sometimes you must dig beneath the surface to unravel authentic temperament. If you value friendship, it should not be time-consuming to learn about each other. Think about guns, deer, hunting, motorcycles, parties, and horses. He is an ombudsman. My bad, he is an outdoors man, who would die if he had to stay inside. Always wants to go somewhere or do something.

Devie Freeman has also a peaceful side that is the resemblance of Canton, Mississippi. A historical, antique but tranquil city. There are days that we would share the same struggle. We also share the same running event. There are days I would teach him how to make curry chicken, so that he can go back to Canton and advertise that he knows Caribbean delicacies. My fondest memory of

Devie does involve curry chicken. One day I told Devie that he could involve potatoes and carrots in the dish to make it look beautiful. I left the pot for one hour. When I came back, there was a terrifying look on Devie's face. So apparently, he did two things wrong. Even Stevie Wonder could have seen that was not curry chicken. He implemented way too many potatoes, and he implemented them way too early. So the curry chicken became a broth. There were more potatoes than chicken. It was as if the chicken was engraved in a cave inside the potatoes.

If Devie was a biologist, he would not believe in semipermeable membrane, which basically means a filter. A spade is spade for him, and I can respect that. He can be considered as the janitor for 324-F. He cleans the bathrooms, living room, and washes the dishes that aren't even his. His wife is going to love him. There is not a doubt in my mind that he is going to make it in life. He has a persistent indication of a successful person. The biggest thing I learned from Devie was through a Bob Marley song. He sang it every day. "Don't worry about a thing because every little thing is going to be all right."

On the beautiful shores of the picturesque Turk and Caicos island laid a young Nigerian boy. His name originates from the Igbo tribe. Meaning, nothing is impossible with God. His name is a tad bit hard to pronounce because of the number of syllables. Ifeanyichukwu Otuonye is indeed my brother. When I think about parkour and a high-pitched enduring laugh, Ifeanyi comes to mind. Turks and Caicos is his fortress. A playground full of opportunity for his marine-life culture. His blood is embedded into the deep blue seas, where octopuses reside among other unfamiliar sea creatures. He lives for the ocean.

We went to the same high school in Saint Elizabeth Jamaica, Munro College. We share similar stories along the way of The Journey. So our stories are relatable. The pain and sacrifices made through our collegiate years are homogeneous. The biggest thing I have learned from Ifeanyi is not to be mediocre. Why be mediocre when you have the opportunity to be great?

The friendship that we have developed over the years has camouflaged itself into a telepathic state. I know he has my back, and I know he means good and that's rare.

He has the potential to be in the *Guinness Book of World Records* for food or something related to eating. He has a rambunctious appetite. I think that the same food-eating attitude reflects his hunger for success. A hard worker who is willing to go the distance at the expense of any difficulties. Very goal-oriented and disciplined individual. The decisions he makes are far beyond his age and capability level. He is able to distinguish priorities from wants. He has the brain of a Harvard student. A very smart, business-savvy, computer-oriented individual. He knows how to analyze complex theories in a simplistic and quick manner.

I have watched this young Nigerian boy develop into an elite A class Turks and Caicos long jumper. More importantly, I have watched this Nigerian boy transform into a man. To see the metamorphosis of a caterpillar into a butterfly, is mind-boggling. He will travel the world and have an impact on a multitude of people. Ifeanyi was born in Nigeria, lived in Turks and Caicos, Montserrat, and Jamaica. He also owns a British passport.

Now the third brother is the youngest, the baby of the group. He originates from Kingston, Jamaica. His autonym reveal itself as Javier Lowe. He almost got kidnapped as a baby. Grew up without a father figure. His mother manipulates both roles.

There is a place in Jamaica that goes by the name of Hundred Lane. It is said that one hundred men were killed in this area. As a juvenile, this was Javier's backyard. An environment that was destined for failure. Marijuana, drugs, and ammunitions were at his disposal. Many sleepless nights, where thinking was a debacle. The only solution he had was sports. It was his rice and peas. It was his survival. One of the purest things ever to grace this earth, is a mother's capability to love regardless. This attribute holds no bearings. Javier's mother is a strong black woman. I have only had minimal conversations with her, but it is not hard to distinguish genuine from fake. She has the realm of an authentic personality.

Her tenacity has made it possible for her son to retrieve opportunities. In spite of a macabre environment, he got a full scholarship to Kansas State University and now is a resident of 324-F. An environment that is destined for success.

Personality wise, he is a game connoisseur, vibes master, and the ladies' man. It is very important to me to play the role of a big brother to fill the void of an absentee father. Sometimes Javier make mistakes, but that is okay. Thich Nhat Hanh, a Vietnamese Buddhist monk whom Dr. Martin Luther King Jr. nominated for a Nobel Peace Prize, said, "Understanding is love's other name." That is why I am here to guide him. I understand his upbringing. I am glad that we met each other. It is such a blessing when you can meet an individual who truly cares about your well-being without a hidden agenda. That invigorates a sense of self-purpose within self. Certain things you can't buy within this lifetime. Our friendship is one of those things.

Sometimes homework isn't thought about in 324-F, and sometimes stress is not a factor. We escape all our problems in this home. We have a word that we use heavily. This word is "Gideon." Gideon represents everything outside the door of 324-F. It represents outside noises or the outside world. Gideon can also be a place where you have to face your fears and tackle your problems. It is a place you have to do face-to-face interaction with your fears and also do treacherous hours of school work. The room 324-F is the opposite of that, where the only thing you face is good vibe. The room 324-F is a place that accepts you as who you are and a place where your problems become obsolete. If

324-F was an ornament, it would be definitely a treasure because it captures precious life qualities that are hard to find in the real world.

My bona fide brother was Dane Steen. He was the first Jamaican I met in Kansas. A self-proclaimed baller. He thought that he was Cristiano Ronaldo. He and Ifeanyi would often argue whose brain was better. He is indeed a smart individual and knows how to get out of complex situations. I have witnessed his struggles in Kansas, and I am so proud of the way he overcame them. Definitely a source of inspiration that aid me to become a better Kaneil. A comedic personality with a high value in consciousness. When you are going through problems, you need a Dane Steen in your life.

As a kid, in his summertime, he usually spends time with some family members in the ghetto. He slept in a one bedroom with a room filled with cousins. There was a big yard where he played soccer with the kids in the community. Even though he was in the ghetto, he enjoyed it. Even though it was the ghetto, he was mindful of the advancement of self, making it better for himself and Peaches. Peaches is his mother. Proud to say that he got a dual bachelor's degree in construction science and physical science. He now has a wonderful job in Florida. Those are the type of people who I had to surround myself so that I can also be better.

Then I met another Jamaican who changed my life. It was as if God was putting positive people in my life. His name was Sanjay. A twenty-three-year-old professor, who was teaching at the university. He was teaching microbiology. If you see him, you would never know that he was a teacher. You can never judge a book by its cover. A very vibrant and positive personality. I learned countless valuable lessons from him. He taught me that one hand can't clap and that no man is an island. It's very funny how a stranger can have so much impact on your life. He grew up in Spanish Town, Jamaica, and went to Jose Marti High School. An environment that can be hostile at times. His tough upbringing motivated him to become a better person.

In the deep trenches of Portmore, Saint Catherine Jamaica, lays a beautiful matriarch. A mother who has the attribute to love endlessly. This mother produced two beautiful babies, more specifically twins but with distinct characteristics. They never had much growing up, but their mother worked relentlessly hard to make sure they were all right. We share similarities in terms of the struggle. They originated from a place where five minutes away, hookers sell their bodies at night for a low fraction of a penny. In other words, prostitutes. This can be also related to Maslow's hierarchy. The prostitutes on the streets suffered so much that the only alternative they had was to sell their bodies. Their bodies were a price tag rather than a temple.

Portmore, Saint Catherine, is a humid place with a barrage of mosquitoes. It sometimes has a dry topography. The barren environment was a reflection of the twins' mother's bank account. So things were rough. Regardless of the environment they were in and the financial burden their mother had to overcome, they never allow their environment to determine who they are or who they wanted to become.

They go by the name of Shardia and Shadae Lawrence. They both attend Kansas State University.

Shardia, now Big 12 champion in the triple jump, and Shadae, now a NCAA collegiate champion in the discus. The twins are crucial part of The Journey. Very important in the Caribbean environment. It took me hours or perhaps several days to configure what to present about them. When you're dealing with diamonds, you have to take precious time. "Have you ever watched the movie *Blood Diamond*?" This is a movie, where a fisherman, a smuggler, and a businessman go to the extreme for the possession of a priceless diamond. That is definitely what I would do for the twins. I would go to the extremes for them. Explaining their character need to be handled with delicate care and compassion, just like a diamond.

They are beautiful queens inside and out. They are the embodiment of a natural human being. They are genuine souls with relentlessly caring capacity. If hearts could look like human beings, it would certainly look like them. Writing about them brings tears to my eyes. I honestly truly have a special type of love for them. I am not talking about boyfriend and girlfriend type of love or husband and wife type of love. My love represents more than that. I am talking about a real, authentic, godlike love. When I see them, I don't see sexual symbols. I see sisters. It's funny how a teammate can become a sister. It's funny how a stranger can become family. Talking to them makes my day brighter. They are my sisters, and I thank God that we crossed path, because without them The Journey would be impossible.

We have a special type of relationship where they would just come in and take anything from our cupboards. Our homes are reciprocals. Our mothers are reciprocals. This is what the Caribbean environment is all about. Both of them have an affluent personality that will definitely take them a long way in life. The rich positive vibes they possess and endure makes life worthy of living.

Anything they ask for is automatically a yes.

I taught Shardia how to drive a car, like how any big brother would. She taught me how to remain steadfast and have faith in my dreams, like how any little sister would. Sometimes they feel as if I have an ulterior motive by treating them nice. I think the absence of a father figure trigger that thought because it's something they are not accustomed to. Also the fact that men are treating women without sexual connotations is rare. I love them. They make me feel like Kaneil and not Kaniel Outis. Hopefully, after reading this, they will truly understand that I simply respect them. I will die for them. When I say die, I don't mean suicidal mode. I don't mean killing myself. It's a rhetoric. I will go to the extent to fight for them, and if in the process of fighting for them, I die, then so be it. Respecting women has become fossils, a petrified state, where rape is now trending. Any malicious intent catered toward them, by anybody, will be confiscated on my accord.

A big sister has the subscription of fervor. The prayers of a bigger sister were answered through the Caribbean environment. I have always wanted a big sister. When I was younger, I thought, if I had a bigger sister it would enable me to have more girlfriends. A concept that rise from frivolous thinking. Clarendon, Jamaica is the home of the Milk River Bath, a mineral spa famous for the therapeutic purposes. Kimberly Williamson was from Clarendon.

She was a very ambitious sister. She has the personality of a go-getter. She was NCAA champion in the high jump. A very talented individual. Her personality may come off as condescending because she tells the truth, no matter who you are, and I can respect that. She is really an incredible and playful person at heart.

Her smile is radiant, and she is important in the Caribbean environment.

You have a Jamaican proverb that goes like this: "Wi neva born wid gold spoon in a wi mouth." This means that we were not born in luxury and had a rough life. We never had handouts. To see a girl coming from a place of struggle, to see her grow coming from Frankfield, Clarendon, now completing her master's degree, is an amazing blessing. To see a journey suffices through another individual, it gives you hope.

Can you guess which island I am about to describe? An island with coral reefs and sandy beaches is a divine canvas for the pupils of the eyes. It is a warm experience to witness the Caribbean Sea. A land of indigenous and colonial artifacts. A snorkeler's paradise, engulfed in hydrographic lifestyle. In the eyes of the insignia lies the sun, which represents the dawning of a new era. The red indicates the energy of the people, blue is hope, and the black represents its African ancestry. I am talking about the island of Antigua and Barbuda. There lives another sister.

Strong built and a shot-put thrower for Kansas State University.

Jess St. John comes from the shores of the leeward islands Antigua and Barbuda. She is a very charismatic and humble individual. She is one of the coolest person I have ever met. Proud to call her family. She has genuine characteristics of a noble person. A very business-minded individual and has many fruitful ideas.

I have never seen any other individual love his or her own country so much. She loves the people of Antigua. She takes pride in her culture, and I take pride in our friendship.

Then we had the statuesque Barbadian queens: Akela Jones and Sonia Gaskin. Such wonderful persons. Akela Jones can wine down low to a soca beat. The meaning of the word "Bajan" is down low so you know she can dance. However, she can jump up high over any high-jump bar. NCAA champion in the heptathlon. Sonia Gaskin—nobody would ever think of hurting her. She is the definition of pure. She has richness in kindness. Then there was the transformation of the Africans. Wurrie Njadoe from Gambia, Rhizlane Siba from Morocco, and then a few other Americans. Everybody was engaged in the Caribbean spirit. It was a monopoly. The exclusive position of positive vibes. Big up to Shirtman, Mitchi Don, Pele, Jullane, Akia, Renae and Shanae Mckenzie.

I used to watch my grandfather make a strong drink, a nonalcoholic drink! Supligen, oats, dragon, carrot, peanuts, just to name a few apparatuses. When you see a grandfather with a blender, it's a powerful thing. The passion in which he makes such a drink is far from melancholy. It is a jubilant feeling to see the process of a healthy substance. It is a jubilant feeling to know that you are in a healthy environment. The way I dealt with Kaniel Outis was through my Caribbean environment. As readers, it is important for you to understand that. There is a thing in science that is called "autophagy." This happens when the cells in the body rebuild themselves. The process of autophagy strengthens the cell. It's a renewing system. It's a wonderful thing, and that's the way how I conceptualize the Caribbean environment. The Caribbean environment was a process of autophagy.

Imagine a sea without water, a woman eyes without tears, because all the pain is inside. A Saudi Arabian girl was raped every day for six months. She has minimal logic. She classifies herself as a mannequin. Her head is held down in disdain for this world. She found a way to run away from the rebels, got captured, and migrated to a counseling hospital in Germany. In her mind to have an afterlife is fictitious. Someway, somehow, she still finds a way to start a new journey. Her communication is done through drawings. She is at a current stage where she is smiling. She decides to start living again, but she lives with deep scars. She said that she has pain, and it's like one hundred deaths! Yet she is searching for reconciliation of hope. Everybody has a Kaniel Outis stage in their life. Do not tell me you can't change your circumstances. There is always a way; even a ruined Saudi Arabian girl sees that. Her new environment was positive psychologists in the German hospital, so different from the rebels who raped her. A positive environment is important! It is a vital source of strength.

# Chapter 5: The Cliff

Imagine a nonliving thing with a generic human emotion—a needle in a haystack screaming for help. Sometimes it's not always sunshine and rainbows. My perspective has changed through the Caribbean environment, but my predicaments remain the same. When it rains, it really pours. Premature premonitions are a cancer, nothing symbolic to have. When you look at the characteristics of a cliff, you think about a gigantic vertical rock caused by erosion or weathering. That is not the type of cliff I am talking about. Nanga Parbat is the ninth highest cliff in the world. Located in Pakistan, Nanga Parbat can also be described as a difficult climb. The synopsis of The Cliff exuberates my relationship with my collegiate coach—a difficult climb. In fact, there was no relationship. As things got better with my environment, things got worse with my coach. It's like I can never have my cake and eat it. It is a frustrating thing when you can't communicate with your present coach, especially when your previous coach was literally your father.

A train ride can make you visualize an eternal future. A bumblebee sucks from a sunflower for potent energy. A baby sucks from the mother's bosom for milk to gain nutrients. It's a peaceful state to enjoy the journey, but sometimes you don't know where the train goes. We live in a vermillion universe—a place where there is the danger of neglect. It's not easy to go on without zeal. Due to a weak source of encouragement, Inertia comes into play.

My track accessories were no longer a by-product of happiness. The spandex, singlet, and spikes were like dinosaurs. A scary thing to have, because I would lose in them. The track was no longer a citadel. I felt like an actor in *The Maze Runner*, trying to survive. It is a scary thing to see an oblique future with no reparation—the thought that births from a neglected soul. I thought that I was a mannequin because my coach would just walk by.

My respect for coach was like an Egyptian castle, at the highest level. However, our relationship was like Pythagoras's theorem—difficult. It was bizarre. He does not even know most of the things in this book, because we didn't speak. Our relationship needed some type of adhesive. For four years our communication patterns were incoherent. This is the thing, though. He is a very hard worker, a dynamo, and a very organized person who always writes workouts. I used to wonder when does he sleep. He was a track guru, a high-jump kingpin, and coached several Olympians. But, I thought that he never had the time for me. My significance was insignificant because I wasn't producing current goods. I was running slow, not because I was slow but because of external factors. He would never sit down and take the time to have a conversation—an actual conversation, not a mandatory meeting. Maybe if he had spent one second and asked how was my day, I wouldn't drop even a millisecond off my time.

To shun a dream is to negate light. To close a curtain is to give up. These are uncharacteristic of a coach. Do you judge a coach by how much championship he or she wins? That is what's trending in the NCAA. Nobody wants to take the time out and grow and build. Instead of flour, coaches want cake. Everybody wants readymade athletes who can score instantly. The journey of a fertilized crop from soil to harvest takes time. Only a few wants to take the time and invest in athletes. Some people only see their job as a pay grade, instead of a passion. Some coaches have bravado egos, which is innutritious for a struggling athlete.

Track and field is a self-disciplined sport. It first starts with the athlete. Discipline is then a necessity. It's not how you start the season, it's how you finish. Anyone can start something, but the key is consistency. I must be honest. Sometimes I can be mocked by my own morals. Meaning, I am human, and we do make mistakes. Mistakes such as going to bed late at nights or not eating healthy. It was easy for me to recognize that and go back into a prime meridian. You can't be afraid of the truth. It's the first state of reconciliation.

One thing I am sure of is that I trained hard. Well, everybody can say they train hard, but at the training I wasn't afraid to die. Honestly, I was not afraid to get into a deep state of lactic acid from early. I pride myself on the effort, regardless of what was going on in my life. But the effort without encouragement is stifling. For four years I did not miss one training session, I did not disrespect anyone, stood in my lane and paid the toll, even when there was a detour. One time my coach looked at me and said that maybe I am trying too hard. I thought about it for a second, and then I wonder is that really such a bad thing.

On a serious note, I never thought I could talk to my coach. It was like an opaque wall. I used to just deal with the repercussions of him not knowing about his athlete. Five more minutes at the start of training session was all I ever wanted. At times I could not relay that message to him. One of the worst things was to get injured because if you're neglected while you're healthy, imagine if you're hurt. I have had injuries before, and he would just rush me back, so I could run 4 × 400 at the championships.

From aisle one to fourteen, there is vacancy. I thought Walmart had everything. A relationship with a coach was never to be found. They say that the ramification of my subpar performance is mental. How can it be mental for four years? I always thought that the concept was rubbish. I always thought that I had a strong positive mind anyway.

My asset in track was that I have a super recovery rate. I breed on speed endurance. My coach was coaching me as a power sprinter. So it was a paradoxical effect, and there was no improvisation. Honestly it felt as if he didn't care about me. It was as if after my eligibility was done, our scarce conversations had an expiration date.

Some things are just never said. Some things just goes unknown. Great potential is one of those things. Respect to all the student athletes who just attempt to try. Respect to all the student athletes who coaches would ignore. Respect to the student athletes who wants to graduate to make their family proud. If you actually look close enough, you can see the great things that people do. The neglects and rejects are people too; nobody fully understand this, but I do. We all are champions in our own little way, but the problem is that nobody celebrates us. An ordinary person is powerful, and it's just that their deeds go unrecognized. The word "celebrity" is overrated. We can add a whole new dimension to this, in terms of societal context. Respect to the lady who cooks lunch in a cafeteria. Respect to the man who collects bottles and cleans the streets. Respect to the taximen who hustle for their families. Respect to the background singers. Respect is a form of appreciation. So respect to the readers who are reading this book.

Before race day I would go into a zone, a state of mind preparing for war. A ritual perhaps. It was my anesthetic to prevent pain during uncertainty. The dark blue of the Dr. Dre Beats is cushion over ears. The pressing of "play" on an android device was stigmatic. A beat will come on. I would rewind it like an 800 m. I would listen to inspiring records, hoping to get school records. I was meditating. I usually call my mom for my medication, a dose of inspiration. She would prescribe the drug of positivity. She was my doctor. I would visualize the entire race prior to the actual race. I would visualize winning, but I would never visualize my coach hugging me or telling me that I did a good job. That never happened, so my point of view was always miscued. Every time I stepped on the track, I visualize my family, so my motivation was intrinsic. An umbilical cord gives fetus oxygen; a Beats wireless cord gives me a mental calmness.

Then race day would happen, and I would hear no music. My ritual was discombobulated by my coach's Syracuse attitude. Blue and orange—I thought that he was bipolar. He never encourages me, so my living became nocturnal. Talking to him after a poor performance was like dipping your hands into hot oil or trying to touch the back of a porcupine.

The way I dealt with his wrath was at nights. Remember, I became nocturnal. In the nights I even try to sleep with a hoodie on, to cover me from all the negative things he would say. I would then read *The Odyssey,* the story of a Greek hero. A voluptuous bottle is Coca-Cola. The liquid is dark and acidic but quenching at the same time. To quench means to satisfy. For my satisfaction I would just give coach the benefit of the doubt. You know, let bygones be bygones.

Do you remember the first time you were able to read? Well, some people cannot answer that question because they simply do not remember such a time. Certain processes in life are not automatic. It is an infallible truth, but sometimes children are born without parents, and you wonder how can this be. The responsibilities of parents are often simulated right after the delivery room. Cowards run away from responsibilities, and it is an inhumane gesture to abandon a seed. Through deductive reasoning we can then develop a rationale and state the following: Without nurture and care, a life can be paralyzing, not physical but mental, affecting valuable life qualities, which stifles growth. Neglect is then born, which alters cognitive dissonance.

This in a way can also be applied to collegiate coaches. I think my coach cared only about conference championships. Well, at least that is how it seemed. If he actually cared about me and other struggling athletes, he had a weird way of showing it. If he actually does care, anyone who is reading this book can ask him the question, "Do you know what Kaneil Harrison is doing right now?" If he can answer, it would be a wonderful surprise, or it would be through the grapevine. My point is that his *coaching* stopped immediately after my last race. That is not the definition of a true coach. Listen, I am not sorry for anything I have said, because it is the truth, and I'm supremely sure I know what I have experienced. So do not mistake me for a John Nash with schizophrenia. I indeed have a beautiful mind.

The main problem was that, there was no principle of individualization. He did not treat us like isotopes. Isotopes are atoms with the same number of protons but have a different number of neutrons. So we were all track athletes (similar), but we had different running characteristics and personalities. So it is impossible to coach everybody the same and expect skyrocketing results. The goal of individualization is to capitalize on each athlete's strengths, exploit their genetic potential, and strengthen their weaknesses.

His intelligence quotient (IQ) was abnormally high, but his emotional intelligence (EQ) was abnormally low. A Harvard theorist Howard Gardner stated that, your EQ is the level of your ability to understand other people, what motivates them, and how to work cooperatively with them. I wish that he could have met me somewhere in the middle between IQ and EQ, but you could not get a derivative from my coach. A sensitivity to change, which made my life calculus.

Settling in Addis Ababa and buying property is what rich men do. Settling in a 2001 Nissan Maxima, reading over the lines of this chapter is what I do, hoping that my lines can be subliminal. A can of Red Bull is in the cup holder. I am hibernating. To me some of the lines seem a little subtle. I have no intent to disrespect or slander any character, but I have every intent for my story to be heard. We will walk the same journey. It takes a ferocious spirit to counterattack an autocrat. These are my untainted lines.

For the life of me, I could not understand why I had to run at every single-track meet, especially my junior and senior years of college. I would sometimes compete in more than even three events and my body could not manage it. While running the 400 m, after 250 m, it always felt as if someone shot me from the stands with a semiautomatic weapon, because I always struggle to finish. I was tired week in and week out and my coach could not understand that. My background work was always feeble, so I could never last through a season. My coach treated me like I was a crane, a machine. My body failed to recover time and again, and I got burned out. I found humor in the fact that the number of miles I did in a season add up to the sum of my track scholarship. It is as if every dollar they paid for my tuition, they took it back out of my body.

Sometimes I dream of a life of eating chocolate-chip cookies in Dubai, and sometimes I think of a revenge plot like Angelo DuBois against Cookie. But my mommy grew me better than that. I know better. I cannot let a licentious world curve my charisma or devour my consciousness. I wanted to be like Karisma, a girl who has the heart of a lion, and not Lucious Lyon. So I stand firm through all atrocities.

My real coach was the receptionist in the athletic department. She was my pacifier and firecracker. Strangers can bless your life in a way that the blessing seems so magnanimous. My school wants to talk about diversity and inclusion. She has been working for Kansas State University for twenty-four years; seventeen years with athletics. She has the highest level of education—a PhD for God's sake, and still has only a part-time position. Struggling to make ends meet. Is it because she is black? She has watched others come in and get marvelous positions. The hypocrisy of modern times. I don't care who wants to get mad, but that is the truth. She understands me because she is also a mannequin. We had our own language. A macaronic language. Do you know that you can be a hostage and don't know you're a hostage because you're blinded by the love of your work? She is fifty-seven years old and haven't experienced true euphoria yet. It melts my heart every time I walk in the office and see her cry. Not physically, but her heart cries.

I thought that the relationship between a coach and an athlete was a partnership. I had to learn how to be a sole trader. Remember, we don't live with regrets. So I am grateful for my experiences with my coach. It has taught me how to be patient.

Patience is a virtue. A lot of wisdom has been self-manifested. What I went through has taught me how to be independent and how to make tough life choices on my own. As an athlete, though, you should never have to feel the burden of feeling alone. At that moment in time, it became more than track. It was more about survival as a man. Back then the decisions that I made was all about sacrifices and being able to see the bigger picture. Life is like a game of chess; the moves that you make must be strategic, you must protect your king at all cost. The king is the most important piece. Similarly in life, the king is your soul. This is like an unspoken truth. Many people have asked me the question, "Do you hate your coach?"

A tiger has malicious intent toward its prey. A mother has conscious love toward her seed. I love both the tiger and the mother. I do not have the capacity to hate, because when you hate, you become a different person, which is toxic for you and your environment. Even if a person disrespects me, I still love them, because I am aware of the fact that we are all human beings. Meaning, we are not perfect, and we are susceptible to making mistakes. I will still find it in my heart to help a person who has backstabbed me. I am not stupid, but I am free. Learn to forgive, and do not let hate consume your heart. It is the journey that we go through in life, that has enabled me to think in those lines. So give thanks for the journey, regardless of the current situation. An unfortunate truth, but some people only give thanks on Thanksgiving Day. Always remember this, your predicaments can become testimonies. So never lose yourself. You can't disrespect your core and expect results at the crust.

From a crumbled folder leaf comes memories. I guess I wrote these words some time ago. Call it my exodus. I guess you can call it venting. So here it goes.

*Dear baby girl,*

*I would look deep into your Olympic eyes and hypnotize about what might. Girl, you're in a diamond league. I met you when I was thirteen. Twelve, eleven, ten, and nine seconds, I would watch you. You were my crush, and I fell in love with you. You made my heart beat the fastest. You have two beautiful curves but with stretch marks. I don't care though.*

*You broke my virginity, and I would give you the baton. We would go through rounds. A platonic love. Love it when you give me cake, flowers, and gold medals too. You made me travel the world. I am grateful. In high school we had the best psychiatrist. One that would prescribe all the right medicines. I miss our high-school psychiatrist.*

*I gave you my best, ran fort lets and spend hours on our relationship. There are days that I look at the computer screen and Google your name, just so that I can be better for you.*

*However, why did you make me your ventriloquist? A dummy. I feel like a fool. Feel like I am from Neptune. Sometimes I don't feel any more. I guess men do really cry. You're the first girl to make both my heart and hamstrings hurt at the same time. Sometimes you gave me standing ovations, but sometimes you embarrassed me in front of a crowd. I think you're ungrateful, but I take part of the blame. I can't even blame our psychiatrist in college, even though he prescribes the wrong medicines.*

*At times you get upset with me because I don't eat the right food. I know you are concerned about my health. Sometimes you get insecure when I stay late up at nights, but you never would understand that I was doing school work. You get mad when I speak about Rebecca, but you leave me no choice. My tears are so navigable that I can use it for art. Please draw my tears into an apricot, a fruit that bears the fruit of several species. Please bear several understandings. I am writing to tell you that, maybe you don't have Olympic eyes. Maybe this is a breakup.*

*Who am I to love you and not call you by your name? ...Track and Field.*

*Sincerely,*

*Evolution of a Student Athlete*

# Chapter 6: Man with Tangerine Chevy

Morocco is my birthplace. Somehow, I have forged my way into paint, instead of citrus. My carcass is a Chevrolet. Vroom! Vroom! Exhaust and combustion is exhilarating. It makes my paint glow. My intellect is personification, and my owner is a man of academia. Who am I? I am Tangerine Chevy. Who is my owner? Bernie Hayen, a professor at Kansas State University, who has revolutionized my level of thinking.

After enduring shenanigans with my coach. All I could think about is just finishing school. Apparently, this athlete thing was not working out. You know a sense of graduating. Focusing on the book aspects. It was my junior year of college, and I just did not know what to do. I think I needed therapy. The student-athlete experience for an immigrant was inhumane. Life was a pressure. It was like wearing the number-ten jersey for the Brazilian national team or being the victim of a vegetable in a soup. Even though I chose to focus all my energy into school, I view the school system as such.

1798, surrounded by sucrose and the Atlantic. Don't mistake the Atlantic as an ocean. It's my tears with an archipelago of confusion. Don't mistake sucrose as sweetness. It's my acrid "job." I count the sweat on my face every day. I have fifty-six hundred droplets on my skin. Where am I? Somewhere in the Caribbean. Maybe Columbus can tell you. I am cutting sugarcane, and it's not really that sweet. The only thing that is sure in my world is tyranny and a genocide holocaust. The surest thing of all is being a slave. So I find pleasure in just counting my sweat. Now, I have 5,601 droplets on my skin. What if I told you I am not actually sweating? But the droplets are my master's spit. I would travel the world, not as free as a pigeon but as a peon, that my master would pee on. To escape from reality, I need a submarine of prayers.

To the white man, "How can you molest my mind just to get molasses for profit?" I remember traveling. Not to Paris, France but to the Bermuda Triangle. I see ships, chains, and other people like me. I hated the isosceles triangle because I would figure out two side of my problems, but then there was melanin. I needed an equilateral. To get that I guess I have to be born again. I am not speaking as a reincarnated Kaneil, but I am speaking for my great grandfather who never had a voice—the one whom I have never met, who was a slave. Call it my tribute. It is such a shame this is still happening. If you don't believe me, then Google "Libya."

I say all that to say. School reminded me of slavery—locking and confining our minds into a horrific chamber. The professors have sex with our minds without a condom, leaving behind the virus of ignorance. Instead of just regurgitating facts and figures to just pass an exam, I needed something different. I needed to actually learn. John Nash said that, classes will dull your mind and destroy the power of true authentic creativity. Then I met someone, a professor who stimulated my intuition and cared about my holistic development. Apparently, John Nash was wrong. He did not care about exams, but he cared about educating my life through various deontological topics. His name was

Bernie Hayen. Bernie means "as brave as a bear," no wonder he was the first and only professor to tell me the truth. This professor symbolizes how I made what I was learning in the classroom, applicable to my life.

Before I delve into how one professor changed my life, there is one more thing I would like to say to my ancestors. I remember back in the day, when as kids, we used to carve out orange-juice boxes into trucks, so we could have them as toys. Also remember carving out part of the coconut tree into a cricket bat so we could play outside. Remember putting up four stones as soccer goals to play scrimmage on the street side, making paper planes, and paper boats. Now all that people think about is the paper. Climbing and picking fruit trees on the country side was gratification. In the Caribbean, as kids, we never had the privilege of rollercoasters, but our life was a rollercoaster. Nevertheless, we treated everything like Disneyland. A land of marble, hopscotch, dominoes, fancy storytelling, and Sunday ball game. The nineties was good for my fellow ancestors. It is through those medium I have learned a variety of traits. It is my roots and chalice; my roots and culture. The old days.

Now everybody lives in Mark Zuckerberg's backyard. We have Instagram, Facebook, and Snapchat now. Social media has taken over. A place where people flaunt a rich life, but they are broke in real life. A place where people love "likes" instead of loving one another. Instead of family conversations around the dinner table, we now have iPhones. There are fidget spinners and hoverboards. A man is not hot, and people find pleasure in a man who sprinkles salt on red meat. A cop's car siren doesn't mean safety, especially if you're black or Hispanic. So you see much has changed, but much has not changed.

Now back to schedule. Chrysanthemum, dandelion, orchids, hibiscus, dahlia and sacred lotus are beautiful flowers. Amazing glorification for the eyes of a living creature. A botanical garden is pulchritudinous. To see sunlight kiss the petals and water hug the seeds brings out the rainbow in the sky—the token of the covenant that God made with Noah. As a kid, my mother would take pride in watering her garden. As a college student, my professor Bernie Hayen took pride in ensuring that I learned. The detailed elucidation of flowers, is not only there to serve a captivated mind but also to show that Bernie Hayen is homogenous to a florist.

He makes seeds grow.

Jamaicans are always late. My first encounter with Bernie was at the first class of a new semester. I was late. He was the first professor who knew my name before introduction. He told me that I was from Jamaica. He told me that he enjoyed beef patties, Wray & Nephew white overproof rum, reading the *Gleaner*, and taking the JUTC bus while in Jamaica. I was like, "Who in the world is this?" I was aghast and impressed by his encyclopedic knowledge. On the first day of class being late, the last thing I expected was a professor to know my biography. From our very first conversation, I knew that he cared, and because of that thought concept, he had my undivided attention for the rest of the semester.

This may sound psychedelic, but I figured out how to improve my life through various themes that a professor was teaching in the classroom. It is a humane thing to know what's right. It's a burning concept that we all know, but oftentimes gets camouflaged with what we want to do. And that's the notion of ethics. That was the nature of Bernie's class. Through Bernie Hayen's class, I have fantasized with multiple aspect of ethics, and it had led me to a Maya Angelou video on YouTube.

It was Dr. Maya Angelou who said the following words: "I'm doing my best to live what I teach. You don't really have to ask anybody the truth; the truth may not be expedient, it may not be profitable, but it will satisfy your soul. It gives you the kind of protection that bodyguards can't give you. Try to be the best you can be, to be the best human being. Try to be that in your church and in your temple. Try to be that in your classroom. Do it because it is right to do. People will know you and they will add their prayers to your life. They will wish you well. Try to live your life in a way that you will not regret years of useless virtue, inertia, and timidity. Take up the battle. Take it up! It is your life. This is your world."

Bernie gave me a new world. A world where I was so focused that everything started working right. Not to say things were perfect, but because of him I was living right and had the right values,

heights of great men reach and kept. So I started working day and night, toiling through the night to be the best version of myself. Man with Tangerine Chevy is the opposite of Kaniel Outis, a cascading series of good activities.

I started getting accolades and recognitions. Achievement such as Big 12 Champion for Life. Big 12 Champion for Life is a campaign highlighting life-changing stories through the opportunities that a scholarship provides. The young women and men given opportunity to compete in their chosen sport, embody the defining characteristics of a champion: leadership, perseverance, community, service, and discipline. My track times started getting better. I got on the commissioner's honor roll. My GPA for the semester was 3.75. On top of that gained Academic All-Big 12 second team.

Instead of just loafing around in business classes, I started taking notes. I fell in love with eBay. I started selling personal items, and I realized I was good at it. Because of my marketing class, I realized I could do more. Then I took it up a notch. I started contacting wholesalers from Indonesia, Hong Kong, and Taiwan, operating as a retailer, selling various items, from clocks and watches to apparels, exporting products to as far as Denmark, Russia, and South Africa. Because of my accounting class, I learned more about financial ratios and took pride in my ROI. In a short time span, I made a little over $10,000 in total sales.

Don't get me wrong, I'm not telling you all of this to show off, but only to encourage someone who is reading this book, that it is possible to turn things around. Words are powerful, and the greatest thing that happened to me was that I was inspired by a professor.

Everything just started to skyrocket. I got involved with online charities. I used 10 percent of my eBay sales to donate to children's hospitals. I went on an amazing life-changing experience to Nicaragua with K-State Athletics Cats across continents. The trip was used to help build a multipurpose sports court so that kids could get to play. An amazing experience where I found out more about myself. I also got the opportunity to bond with amazing student athletes. It is amazing to see a group of random student athletes transform into family. I have huge respect and love for every person on that trip.

In Nicaragua it was hard work. Mixing cement, shuffling stones, and maneuvering wheelbarrows. Instead of a bathroom, we had bushes; instead of a bath tub, we had a hose. We were surround by domestic animals. We were away from the outside world—no phones or Internet—away from first-world problems.

Even though it was hard, it was fun, and I loved it. We took pleasures in the simplicity of life. It is such a blessing that you can wake up in the morning and just get a cup of coffee. Things like jumping into a Lagoona or just seeing a smile on kid's face are electrifying. As humans we must realize that nothing in life is a guarantee and every day is a blessing. That's why you should laugh and smile more regardless of the journey. Live in the moment and be grateful for everything.

It is such a blessing when you can go into a new environment and feel loved. It was as if God gave me a second chance with soccer. I am now working with Kansas State Women's Soccer as a student manager.

One of the smartest girl I ever met was from Iceland. I met her through a new soccer environment. Her country is like a precious stone, containing fascinating geysers and hot springs. Her wisdom is uplifting and decorative for the room of one's mind. It is good when you can go into a new environment and instantly find friends who can motivate you. She has become a lifetime Nordic friend. She goes by the name of Steinunn.

The opportunity the coaches have given me has been a life-changing moment. I have nothing but love for the coaching staff.

Mike Dibbini, Jessica Smith, and Gabe Romo, the coaches of Kansas State Women's soccer, has certainly changed my life for the better. The wisdom they possess is mind blowing. They have certainly painted a positive canvas in the depths of my mind. While working with them, I met someone, someone whom I believe in so much, probably even more than myself.

Sometimes I elevate my body into an upright spiral to touch the stars, not necessarily to touch it but to reach for it and put it in someone's pocket. Not for me, but as an inspiration for someone else. Like a cop reaching at maximum fingertips for a suicidal victim, alongside an unpaved precipice, I reached for a broken hand. Gas stations are for car engines, but my fuel is altruism.

To serenade my enthusiasm, I searched for a sulfur rock, a Korean melon, and an omelet. I am searching for things that are yellow. The revelation of a substitute product for the downfall of not reaching the stars. So I improvise. Yellow is a color of positivity. There was a Mexican girl on the soccer team who needed every yellow. As Dora would say, amarillo. Along with the faith of a

pumpkin seed. Dora Gallo, meaning "God's gift."
When people look at her, they saw Yugoslavia. A
country that is no longer existent. When I look at
her, I see Qatar—a wealth of talent.

From the very first time I saw her play soccer,
her skills were monumental.

She wasn't an
average player,
but she was
playing average.
Many people did not believe in her because of her
incapacitations. She had low self-efficacy and very
poor stamina, and that's why she looked ordinary
on a soccer field. I believed in her so much that it
would keep me up at nights. I believed in her so
much that I would have an inner tear, every time

she does not play. I would stay up late in the nights to think of ways she could get better. Her problem was my problem.

I have watched her cry, and I have watched her work insidiously hard. Regardless of what was going on in her environment, we work every night so that she could get better. Each day I witnessed growth in her attitude and tenacity. My ultimate goal with her was beyond the dimensions of soccer. If I got her better in soccer, it would be a blessing, but that wasn't the objective. My objective was to get her better as a person and to develop her into a wonderful human being. Soccer was bonus. Every day I was teaching her life lessons through soccer. I wanted her to be better than the Dora yesterday. We have gotten so close, and I am proud to call her family. I have nothing but love for her, and I will never give up on her. This may sound weird, but I think I met Dora for a reason. Sometimes God position people in your life so that you can be the best you. Sometimes we can never understand the journey, but the journey has a reason.

I am glad that I have met her. It is because of her I realized the fulfillment of my dreams. I realized what I want to do. I wanted to be a collegiate soccer coach. How am I sure? When you have a passion for something, you no longer need an alarm clock. It becomes a part of your subconscious. In order to help someone, you first must understand his or her personality.

I realized that she loves to paint. The reason why

she loves painting is because it gives her a chance to connect with inner passions. It keeps her in line with her artistic style and creative being, which is important to her. That's why if she is bored, she will find creative ways of entertaining herself, doing simple things such as tie-dye or scribbling in a book.

Sometimes she can see life with no color. Meaning, sometimes in life she may be lost, and she blames herself. When she is in love with someone, she will think the world makes sense and will do everything to promote his dreams. The worst thing a person can do to her is ignore her; it challenges her sensitivity. She values a listening audience. The same appetite she has for cheese, is the same she has for helping people. Her heart is guarded because of previous encounters, so she doesn't trust easily.

Watching Dora praying for her food is so divine, an eloquent appreciation of nourishment. It is as if it was her last prayer on earth. A sense of appreciation is so beautiful. An infinite thing is powerful—things like love, compassion, and appreciation. It is amazing to see all three qualities in one person. The female Ronaldinho Gaucho in my books.

I am proud to tell you about Bernie Hayen. I have experienced the feeling of being in a black cape. No, I am not talking about Darth Vader. No, I'm not talking about Batman. I am a Kansas State University graduate, graduating with a bachelor of science in business management.

I have watched the jubilation on my mother's face as she watches me collect my diploma. To *know* that I make my mother proud and happy is a splendiferous feeling. I know that it is impossible to repay her with anything, because she gave me birth. The way she made me feel is how Ray Hudson feels when commentating about soccer.

Ray Hudson's commentary: "Oooooooooh! Messi! Messi! Flings his flaming spear in the hearts of Real Madrid. Beautiful counterattack. Messi born was in a cross-fire hurricane, and he is a jumping jack flash. You can drop a tarantula in his shorts, and he will still be cool. Demonic skill. Picks the right pass out of the pocket. Jordi Alba sells it, and Messi catapults it home. A man with the feet of God. Playing poker with a witch, you're going to lose. Messi steps aside and says, *Vamanos, muchacho,* and Neymar stands up to the pressure. It kisses the upright with love. The touch is like a lover's kiss. Absolutely brilliant! How do you describe that? Astonishing. Kaboom! He has

Gramoxone in his body, which belongs to a tiger. Messi is astonishing again.

"Are you kidding me? This is not just a dream. It is a wet dream of orgasmic proportions. This one deludes everybody; it seduces everybody in Real Madrid fan club, and that's for sure. The wonder strike from Cristiano. This got more curves to it than a Jessica Rabbit on steroids."

Ray Hudson's passion in commentating is an understatement in how much I love my mother.

My current state is that I have absolutely no idea what I'm going to do next. I have dreams of going to graduate school to better position myself for my dream job, but I don't know if my parents can afford it. I'm looking through ways and efforts to figure things out. Nothing is concretized. Everything is up in the air right now, but I am not worried because my faith is not in man. It is in God.

I will be forever fearless. Do you know why?

Because of what I have learned in the classroom.

Because of the impact of the man with tangerine

Chevy.

# Chapter 7: Untold Stories

In the college athletic system, there are number of untold stories. Athletes go through so much on a daily basis, but nobody really knows. There are some things in life that are called hidden battles. There are some things in life that doesn't come to surface. I thought it would be good to hear from another athlete's perspective. A different journey to enjoy. A different road to learn from. These are their stories:

**Victim #1**

Rumor has it that the hardest thing in life is starting something—one also heard the story of how the grass is always greener on the other side. This is not necessarily true. Take it from me. A small-town island boy, just trying to make a better life, in a country far away from home. My objective here is not to scare you away from your dreams or furthermore lie to you and tell you that it's an easy getaway. In fact, I will encourage you, whoever is reading this, to go and follow your dreams. However, what I will tell you though, is that there are many hurdles to jump over in the race to success.

I attend school at Texas A&M University—Corpus Christi. In all honesty, I did not know that Corpus Christi was an actual place until I landed here. I'm scheduled to graduate in December with a bachelor's degree in kinesiology, and by far these four years have been the hardest and most tested years of my life. They truly have been "the struggle." Being a student athlete does not help the situation either. Let's not even consider the fact that I am international. Well, not yet at least! Let me further explain some of these struggles.

When it comes to collegiate sports, we tend to take in the word "scholarships." Full scholarships to be exact. There is also a saying that once you're on a full scholarship (full ride as athletes say), you don't need to worry about anything else. That is wrong. Full or no full scholarship, you still need money to do things. For example, a full ride technically handles tuition, books, and all athletic fees. To survive, you would still have to find such things as food and our biggest demon, rent money. What makes this situation work is how they limit a lot of the things we can and cannot do. For example, we cannot have any outside sources of money. Sucks to suck when you're already sucking. As an international student, you can get a job. However, the job must be on campus, and you're limited to how much hours a week you can work. So pretty much you're on your own, with your family, if they can assist you, when you run short on trying to pay bills at the end of each month. But being a student athlete, it's honestly too hard to find the time to go to school, train, and have a job. Most importantly taxes. Your scholarship is taxed for foreign national taxes. So from the little money you get back as a refund after everything is paid for, taxes are taken out for you being a noncitizen. The good thing is you do get these back, if applied correctly, but they typically do not come back in a timely manner. So at this point, you're more into a struggling state.

Another big struggle faced is athletics. Well, the drama that comes with athletics. I have been here for four years. And for these four years I have been here, I have been through a total of five coaches and four athletic trainers. Yes! That's not something I expected to go through. Imagine how each coach has his or her own style of teaching, his or her own philosophy, and his or her own programs. Now imagine trying to adapt to that every year for four years consecutively. Imagine trying to deal with something like that psychologically, worse yet physiologically. Trying to not get hurt from doing different programs versus trying to train hard and compete well to save your scholarship. It's a never-ending battle, which really does get tiresome. The struggle of trying to get good grades while trying to perform well. For example, staying up late to do school work, but sacrificing sleep and rest for practice. It's not as easy as it seems!

Coming to America does have its benefits, but sometimes it seems futile when really and truly that we do what we do for a document. Although this document is weighted when you think about it, it is what it is—a piece of paper. It makes one think, is it all worth it? Regardless, I leave you with this—the struggle is real.

**Victim #2**

Oregon, Arkansas, Ohio, Florida, Texas, Iowa, Oklahoma, Kansas, Wisconsin, Alabama, California, and Arizona. These are some of the places I got to experience, because the University of Nebraska gave me the opportunity to travel to these states. Lincoln, Nebraska has some of the nicest people I have ever met.

My home, Jamaica, is nineteen hundred miles away from Lincoln, and the University of Nebraska never once failed to make me feel at home. The University of Nebraska provided everything I needed to be successful in both my academic and athletic endeavors. There was always someone to help me on every single step of the way. The athletic trainers were very helpful in getting me ready for practices and the competition. There were tutors and academic advisers readily available.

There were a lot of challenges along the way, but I was always ready to work twice as hard to get back on my feet. Every time I stepped on that track, I represented Nebraska proudly. Coming from a warm climate, I remember my first winter in Nebraska, and it was terrifying. It was an extremely different culture, but I quickly adjusted to my new environment. I remember the early-morning weight-room sessions and the rigorous training sessions in the afternoon. My coach was a tough cookie, but he got the job done. At first I hated his training and his training philosophy, but if I could go back to freshman year, I would be a lot more eager to work with him. The reason I say that is because once there is trust between an athlete and a coach, the athlete will benefit tremendously.

Nebraska taught me how to be independent and how to work hard for what I want out of life. Being a student athlete is a full-time job, but Nebraska made it more than manageable, and I am proud to be a part of the Nebraska Alumni.

If I could go back to my final year in high school, I would still choose Nebraska. *Go Big Red.*

**Victim #3**
All my life I have been considered a "student

The

">The Journey

athlete," and this label helped to develop me into the person I am today. I try not to switch it up and consider myself an athlete student, because I always feel that at the end of the day, my education will be the most valuable thing to me.

Being a student athlete can be a difficult thing, especially when you are an international student who is from a different culture, speak a different language, and being away from your family. But It is truly a remarkable experience when you become settled in and start understanding the culture. For me, one of the greatest feeling from being a student athlete is when I excel not just on the field but also in the classroom. It is a very rewarding feeling when you get publicly recognized for your achievements on and off the field. I had the pleasure of captaining my soccer team to only its second national tournament berth in the school's history, but I must say that it doesn't even compare to the feeling I got from being an Academic All-American four times in a row.

There are challenges being a student athlete, but as with every good thing in life, the payoff is much more significant. Yes, it is hard when you must manage your time from 6:00 a.m. each day to 11:00 p.m. at nights because of class schedules, practices, and games. Yes, it is hard when you must sit on a bus for a ten-hour journey both ways. Yes, it is hard when all your peers are out partying and drinking, but you can't, because you have a game tomorrow or the day after. Yes, it is hard when your body ache so bad that you don't want to get out of bed. Yes, it is hard when you are pushed to the limit in practice day after day. Yes, it is hard when you are putting in the work and not getting the results. But! That feeling of winning that all-important game trumps everything. That bond that you create with your teammates by being on ten-hour bus ride can last for a lifetime. That moment you get nationally recognized for winning a championship makes all the sacrifices feel like a vacation. And those everlasting memories and stories that you will one day tell your grandkids certainly makes it all worth it.


**Victim #4**

Making a decision on where to attend school was one of the most challenging decisions I have ever made. I was torn between staying home and attending college in the United States. This decision may have been easy for many Jamaicans—who would really want to stay in a poverty-stricken country and give up the chance of living the American dream? After losing two siblings, I wanted to be close to family, but I knew it would be better for me if I studied abroad. I made the decision to stay, and after a year, I realized it was too much, and in order to make my parents proud and graduate college, I had to leave. Being one of the top high jumpers in my country, I had scholarship offer from some of the best universities in the country, but choosing K-State was a no-brainer.

I started my degree here at K-State in the fall of 2014. Being a student athlete here was different than it was back in Jamaica. Here everyone was invested in your learning and progressing (I thought it was annoying, how much we were babied). The athletic department took really good care of us. We had access to computers, tutors, and just a listening ear if we needed it. With the help and support of the department, I was able to finish my degree in three years and started my master's degree. Coming to K-State was the most rewarding decision I have ever made because it allowed me to leave the island girl (constant partying and drinking) behind and realize my true academic potential.

Traveling is something I am very passionate about. I love going different places and exploring the different cultures. Athletics and K-State afforded me that luxury. In my first year at K-State, I was able to travel to places I only dreamed of and create friendships that will last a lifetime. Traveling and competing is another thing I enjoyed, and most of my competition while at K-State was out of state, so we had to take a bus or flight. My most memorable moment since being here was winning my first NCAA title in 2016.

Before experiencing winter here, the other Jamaicans who were here made it seem like a nightmare. The winter of 2014–2015 wasn't as bad as they made it out to be, and I was glad. It was already a struggle trying to function in a new environment with no means of getting around (not to mention I couldn't ride a bike). Coming from an island where public transport was the go-to, it was challenging for me mainly because I grew up very independent, and to be in a new environment where we had to be dependent was tough.

I like going out with my friends and having a good time, and that is one luxury K-State didn't afford us. With no night life and the stress from school and athletics, over time I started disliking K-State, but believe it or not, if I had a do-over, I would be right back there. And honestly, I needed to stay focused on what was important and what could wait. I am grateful for the opportunity K-State gave me: two degrees at no cost, a national title, and friendship bonds that will last a lifetime. For that I will always be a *wildcat*!

**Victim #5**

Before actually coming to Kansas State University, I had been residing with my godparents for about three years for high school. My mother just had too much to handle, and my godfather figured he could take some of the load off my mother. He had been in love with her for years. I don't know if he still is, but he got married while still having these emotions for her. Over the course of living there, I grew more and more uncomfortable. This was all my fault though, so I really couldn't blame anyone but myself. Still, I didn't like the feeling. After graduating the salutatorian of my high school, my principal had really put up an argument with my godparents that she really didn't think I was mature enough to go. In all honesty, I feel like she was right up until now; however, I really think she just wanted me to stay there and do A-levels for the school, to give them a better reputation. She had obviously won them over.

It had even got to a point where my godfather yelled at me and said that if I accepted coming to K-State now, I would regret it, because he would not speak to me. A part of me believed he just said that out of anger, the other really believed him. Ultimately, I took a chance in coming here. And I could not have chosen a better time to come than winter. It was the absolute *worst*. The transition from the Caribbean weather to the winter was a horrible experience, but my efforts to get here wouldn't go in vain because of a little cold. In fact, I had to travel to Nassau, Bahamas prior to arriving to Kansas for my student visa. That was an experience in itself, but not relevant to my experience here at K-State.

I got here on January 3, 2017. That same day I was supposed to catch a flight and arrive by 5:00 p.m. the latest. I missed my flight for the very first time. Never have I ever panicked so much. But there is a God, and he smiled on me that day with his mercy. I was able to catch another flight that same night and get to Manhattan, Kansas, by 10:00 p.m.—no sleeping over in the airport, no more panicking, and I was relieved. When I arrived, one of the coaches was waiting for me as soon as I got off the airplane. On our way to University Crossing, which is where I live now, he asked me if I wanted to go to Walmart to get a few things. Me being my considerate self, told him I would be fine. I thought to myself it was already late and I've already caused a lot of inconvenience for him. It would be best if I just get tonight over with. *Bad idea.*

I had no sheets, no blankets, pillows, nothing. And anyone who lives in University Crossing can tell you that the size of these beds are highly favorable, but the texture! It was a rough night, I should just say. All I had was my airplane blanket that I slept on, and I used it as a blanket that night. In all honesty, I'm glad I came late that night because I later discovered that had I come earlier at

5:00 p.m., I would've stayed with some twins on the team whom I grew uncomfortable with. I ended up with two girls, not a part of the track team, and we got along just fine.

The next morning, when I woke up, I thought I was going to die. The coach who had picked me up from the airport said he would be coming for me around nine o'clock, but he got caught up and arrived at noon. Fortunately for me, that day, one of my roommates made a big breakfast, and I was able to eat. If not, I swear, I would've died of starvation. The first few days, I must say, were rough, but I just was excited to get started on school and training.

My first day of training, I died. I had $8 \times 150$s. As easy as that sounded in my head, with the little background training that I did back home, I was clearly not ready for the workout that day. I didn't vomit, and I never have really, but I felt sick to my stomach after those 150s.

Myself as a person, I consider my eyes to be big. Huge. Enormous. You get my point. I see a lot of things and want them. And I must admit, I thought there were some really cute guys in our team, and I got easily interested. Not to mention being away from my godparents, having my godmother be extremely religious, so I couldn't do much. This freedom felt like heaven. All I could think of was what to do first! Days went by…weeks went by…months went by, and I developed bonds with people on the team, unimaginable and even some, unspeakable. I was excelling in the social aspect of the collegiate lifestyle.

Making new friends, having fun, going to parties, and just doing my own thing. If it weren't for the "brought-upsy" of my godparents, meaning the way I was raised, I definitely could see myself making some even more ridiculous decisions than the ones I have already made, and for that I'll be forever grateful. Training was going okay a few months in, and I had been competing at track meets for K-State now! Some of the trips were long and exhausting, others short and exciting. But at the end of most of the track meets, I left with a bittersweet feeling. Bitter toward the fact that I still was nowhere near where I wanted to be athletically, which in most cases left me feeling depressed. And sweet because 95 percent of the time, I had made improvements in cutting time. Each time would be less than the last time I competed.

While my feelings toward track had been, and still are, fluctuating, because I still have the exact thoughts, it is the academics that mainly stress me out. Yes, I know I mentioned graduating salutatorian, but I'm a hands-on learner. I learn from teachers drilling things into me and giving me ample practice right there and then on the subject at hand. Here in university, they are nothing like that. There are lectures, which aren't half as fun as my high school, and they definitely don't teach me the way I'm used to being taught. So I find myself struggling in most cases, as I am now. I mean, we have tutors, but even so, they aren't enough. You have them for one hour, and you're not having one-on-one sessions, so every other person is trying to get his or her question in, and you only see them about two to four times a week. So that doesn't do me much good either. I just wish I could have my own teacher for most subjects, but reality is I can't.

So I will just have to deal with it and continue with my self-teachings.

Just recently I've actually had a problem. But to speak in truth, college in itself will be problematic. My scholarship was even threatened because of the ridiculous decisions I made under the influence of "the college life." I just hope that things will work out for the greater good, because as I've been taught, where there's God, there's a way. I just need to redevelop my relationship with him because I have fallen off, and I can admit that. I am currently not sure what will happen to me in future regarding myself being a student athlete here at K-State. But as a wise man once told me: if you put in the work, commitment, and dedication, things will play out for themselves for the greater good. He didn't mention God, but he was always there in my subconscious, guiding me. I hope others do not go into college with the same immature mind-set I had when I first arrived here, because it's a very hard path to recover from. Mentally, it's a very strenuous act. Until now I am still trying to find my way to what I'd say is the right path.

I was the girl having sex left, right, and center, drinking underage, staying out until morning and doing all the things I know I shouldn't have done. So please do not be careless, but be careful.

# Chapter 8: Clementine

Do me a favor. We are going to go through an experience. A personal voyage. Grab a pencil, and tango with your dexterity. Get a paper and become Mona Lisa. Draw tangent lines or perpendicular, anything you like. Become mindless of your interpretation of art. Be free! While drawing get intact with the murmurs of your heart, and contact your inner being.

Personally, I am drawing a runway. So that The Journey Airline flight 22 student-athlete experience can have a safe landing.

Ladies and gentlemen, welcome to Clementine International Airport. Local time is 1:00 p.m., and the temperature is 76 degrees Fahrenheit.

I am writing this chapter in an enclosed

bathroom. It is important to me to create a symphony of unequivocal introspection. Clementine is important. Not a joke thing. As my red pen starts to squirt words on the pages, I started to cry. Realizing that my pen wasn't red, but I was bleeding. Bleeding from the rapacious spirit of hands to form words. You see, I am not crying because of hemoglobin. I'm crying because on the outskirts of the bathroom, I could hear my father rehearsing a eulogy.

In 1997 I remember vividly seeing soldiers. Soldiers in crossfire with gunmen. My mother was working at a bank in downtown Kingston, and we were held as hostages. I could hear gunshots as loud as a rape victim. At two years old, I did not understand it, but I knew that it was not a masquerade. That was a bituminous past. I must travel down memory lane, so you can understand Clementine.

I remember days of living in Kingston at a tender age. I would tell everybody that I was from Chisholm Avenue, proud about my community. Five minutes' walk down the street, there was Jackson Road, a road that I would get so much Toto. A Toto is a Caribbean coconut cake that is prepared on a woodfire.

My grandmother made the best Toto. Now, there will be no more Toto! You see, my grandmother died on the journey. I wish Alzheimer was a boxer so that Mayweather could fight him. Clementine represents everything in this book; it's the middle name of my grandmother.

Clementine represents all the chapters in this book. She is the "Passport" of everything.

Clementine represents "The Transition" between my grandmother's first and last name. She went through a long period of "Kaniel Outis." It is because of her I have the possibility of a "Caribbean Environment." She is a jewel across the Caribbean Sea. Because of her it is possible to climb any "Cliff." Google "Clementine," and you will get the definition of something tangerine, which brings out "Man with Tangerine Chevy." If it wasn't for her, there would be no Daddy. If it wasn't for her, there would be no Daddy for Mommy to marry. If it wasn't for her, there would be no "Untold Stories" for *The Journey*.

The weakness in a grandfather's vocal cords, is outlandish. Never seen my grandfather cry before. I have seen him love before. He loved Mary Clementine Harrison with all his heart and more. She died in his arms in a bathroom. Bereavement is unbearable. Listen, excuse me for a second, let me talk about my grandfather's love for grandma. It is unbelievable. There is no other love like it.

The morning grandma died, grandpa wanted to be in the body bag with her. My grandfather ran down the casket, unashamed, unafraid, and unapologetic of any repercussions of getting no more oxygen. He wanted to be with her. Love can be suicidal. Not saying that he is suicidal. His mind was like plate tectonics, expecting a convergent boundary. "When you're married to someone for over fifty years, how do you live without them?" His mind was an apocalypse.

A couple of days after Grandma's death, I called my grandfather on the phone. When she died, I was still in Manhattan, Kansas. There was a pregnant pause on the phone. Then he said, "Kaneil, this hurt so much! I feel numb. I wouldn't wish this to my worst enemy. I don't know what to do with myself. Who is going to wake me up in the morning and make breakfast and give me my tea? Who is going to pick out my church clothes? Kaneil, we were one person. I feel like someone cut me in half. I am 100 percent positive that there is nobody else like her in this world. She was my friend and right hand. Kaneil, Alzheimer is a wicked thing she was fighting for so long. Your grandmother is a fighter. I loved her more than me. I wished that God could take me instead. I have no problem doing barter. Oh God, this is like a sword down a sore throat."

After that, all I could hear was crying. I would listen to him. I would cry too. Sometimes we didn't say anything on the phone, but I could understand his thoughts. The call ends.

Grandma, I know you're reading from heaven. I hope you are proud of me. I have learned a lot throughout life's journey. The most important thing is finding myself to a place of inner peace. The most important thing is *love*. Money is not important. If I don't have money, I know I must not become frustrated, because when you're frustrated, you become ugly, and God doesn't like ugly. I should just live good, treat people right, and respect myself, and then God will open doors for me, and that to me is wealth.

When I went to Jamaica for the funeral, I sit on a stool in Grandma's backyard. Grandpa Leonard lectured me about a good woman, with tears running down his lips. He gave me great advice. He said, "Make sure you look for a girl with interior qualities. Interior qualities are what matters. Make sure you love for the right reasons. Treat her right. You can argue but never disrespect her. Be humble and kind to her. If a woman won't endure with you in your little beginnings, she should not enjoy your riches."

To my grandfather: Get a towel, get a tissue, get up soldier. This is a powerful message from your grandson. Don't you worry, and don't you cry any more. All my life I have looked up to your values and principles, and now it is time for you Grandpa to look up to me. I am telling you that there is no way possible to bring back Grandma. You can still find beauty through life. Love is a continuum. Love is in flowers, the birds, and the bees. Love is bodacious. It is God's grace. Please don't be hopeless. She loved you, and she wants you to be happy. So please do not burden her with your tears. You can stop crying now. Grandpa, through this book you can find a new hobby. I know her body is perishable, but her spirit remains. Her memories are immortal because of this book. The world will know about her and will know that she is a good woman and that you loved her. She is your Clementine. I haven't found a wife yet. I will surely take your advice. Then, maybe I can give you a granddaughter for your eyes only. "4 Your Eyez Only"—J. Cole, "All Eyez on Me"—Tupac Shakur, "Eyes of Jesus"—Grandma, and that's why her first name was Mary. RIP, Mary Clementine Harrison!

*TO BE CONTINUED....*

Kaneil Harrison

# About the Author

Kaneil Harrison is a former track student athlete at Kansas State University. He graduated with a bachelor's degree in business management. Jamaican by birth. He is currently living in Manhattan, Kansas, with hopes of pursuing graduate school. Kaneil has dreams of coaching NCAA Division 1 Women's College Soccer and owning an e-commerce business. Kaneil writes from the heart and hopes that his journey may encourage you.

Made in the USA
Monee, IL
09 April 2021

65265496R00125